FIRST THIS, THEN THAT

FIRST THIS, THEN THAT

THE ENTREPRENEUR'S FOUNDATION FOR SUCCESSFUL BUSINESS GROWTH

LESLIE HASSLER

STRATEGIX PRESS

Dallas, Texas

FIRST THIS, THEN THAT

THE ENTREPRENEUR'S FOUNDATION FOR SUCCESSFUL BUSINESS GROWTH

BY LESLIE HASSLER

Published by:

**STRATEGIX
PRESS**

Strategix Press
16206 Spring Creek Rd, Dallas, TX 75248

Publisher's Cataloging-in-Publication
(Provided by Cassidy Cataloguing Services, Inc.)

Names:	Hassler, Leslie, author.
Title:	First this, then that : the entrepreneur's foundation for successful business growth / Leslie Hassler.
Description:	Dallas, Texas : Strategix Press, [2024] | Includes index.
Identifiers:	ISBN: 979-8-9904475-0-9 (paperback) | 979-8-9904475-1-6 (Kindle) | 979-8-9904475-2-3 (ePub) | LCCN: 2024908382
Subjects:	LCSH: Success in business. | Small business--Growth. | Strategic planning. | Leadership. | Pricing. | BISAC: BUSINESS & ECONOMICS / Entrepreneurship. | BUSINESS & ECONOMICS / Small Business. | BUSINESS & ECONOMICS / Women in Business.
Classification:	LCC: HF5386 .H37 2024 | DDC: 650.1--dc23

Cover design by Yvonne Parks at PearCreative.ca
Interior design and typeset by Katherine Lloyd, The DESK
Indexing by Russell Santana, E4Editorial.com

CONTENTS

ACKNOWLEDGMENTS

To my family, especially my husband, Ed—thank you for giving me the space to verbally process the ideas and concepts we held dear in this book. Your unwavering and unconditional love and support are the foundation that allows me to live and work as the best version of myself. You are always by my side, and I am forever grateful.

To my brother and sister-in-law, Loren and Becky Shellabarger, III—thank you for pre-reading the book, keeping us honest, and ensuring we didn't take ourselves too seriously. Your feedback brought clarity and laughter to the office.

To Rebecca, my dear friend and COO—you may have read this book more than anyone, but your keen eye for detail and relentless focus on our readers truly made the difference. Your challenges to push harder and improve are why these concepts will now inspire and create magic in someone else's life. I couldn't have done it without you.

To Ally Wilson-Nix, our voracious reader and marketing queen—your energy and contributions to this book have been invaluable. You are the driving force behind getting this message into the world, and we're so lucky to have your spirit and talents guiding us. We may keep you on your toes, but you always exceed expectations!

To the remainder of our team, Penny, Alice, Christi, Cheryl, and Kate—you've all played a part in the creation of this book by bringing your geniuses to the table. I have such a tremendous appreciation for you, your work, and the impact we create together.

Thank you to Janica Smith for your expert guidance in bringing this book to life. Navigating the publishing process was a smoother journey with you by our side.

To the mentors who've inspired me through the books I've read—your influence is woven into these pages. The inspiration for *First This, Then That* stems from a core belief that every business owner strives to be better and build something better. Your ideas, wisdom, and lessons have shaped how I see what's possible and approach that journey with our clients.

To my colleagues and friends who love to chat about business—our conversations always leave me energized and ready to return to the arena and lead the charge toward something better. These discussions fuel my passion, and for that, I am deeply thankful.

Finally, to our past, present, and future Your Biz Rules clients—thank you for trusting us as partners in your business journey. Your experiences, challenges, and successes have shaped the knowledge and insights shared in this book. As small business owners, we often find that all we need is an answer to a question or a nudge in the right direction. Your stories remind us of the shared paths we walk, and this book is a testament to that journey, made possible by your active participation.

COMPANION RESOURCES
Ready to Create Real Change in Your Business?

Don't just read *First This, Then That—experience* it! These companion guides will allow you to create real change in your business. We will even give you one for free!

Unlock deeper insights with the *First This, Then That* Book Club Discussion Guide for free!

Engage with thought-provoking questions and practical exercises to help you prioritize, focus, and take action in your business. Perfect for entrepreneurs and leaders ready to turn vision into reality, whether you're reading on your own or with friends. Download the guide to get started.

Transform Ideas Into Impact—Your Roadmap to a Smoother, Faster-Growing Business Starts Here

Purchase the companion workbook for a more in-depth experience implementing these powerful ideas step-by-step. Imagine your business running smoother, growing faster, and giving you more freedom—all within reach. Start turning ideas into impact.

Find your guide & workbook at
www.yourbizrules.com/FTTTcompanion

INTRODUCTION

Howdy! There are probably 101 reasons you picked up this book. Maybe you have a natural curiosity for business, you are thinking about starting your own company, or, like most people, you've figured out that achieving success in your business is more challenging than you thought.

Good business is simple. It just isn't always easy. My journey is no different. After 17-plus years as an entrepreneur, author, and mentor to other small business owners, I've learned a lot. In my own business, I often joke that I have an MBA from the School of Hard Knocks. If a mistake could be made, I've made it. There were opportunities to make mistakes, learn and grow. When winning at business, I would feel on top of the world. When I was learning, some of those hard knocks hurt more than others.

That is one of the reasons I am writing this book for you. Over the years, there are things to learn while on your entrepreneurial journey that you could never have imagined needing to learn. I want to share with you what I have learned and what I share with my clients so that perhaps you can avoid those mistakes yourself.

One of my friends, also a business owner, once went to a multimillionaire to ask him how he became successful. He told her that he simply failed a lot. Every time he failed, he learned more. Although she appreciated the answer, she wanted an easier way to learn. Still looking for answers, she went to a business coach. He was a typical business coach who had a binder to go through. When she finished every page in the binder, do you know what she did with the binder? Nothing. The binder sat on the shelf as an unhelpful, expensive reminder that it was not helpful. At Your Biz Rules™, one of the things our clients find valuable is that while we have a process, we know how to tailor the process and strategies to align with you as the owner, your values, and your vision—no more fixed binders to collect dust—just practical, time-tested advice.

As a team of business strategists, we can not imagine giving answers that feel like a "one-size-fits-all" solution. Every business is different, and each owner is special. Think of what we share as an operating system that takes what you have and improves your business. The system we use meets you where you are and helps you get where you want to be, profitably and sustainably, without the burnout.

This book contains the foundational knowledge needed for businesses to grow, an important part of your journey but often misunderstood. You'll find clarity through chaos. What was once stuck moves freely. You'll avoid mistakes and fast-track profits and growth.

You should know that we care for each business we work with as if it were our own. As a company, we're here to give your instincts and decisions a fresh, objective perspective, often spotting opportunities and paths that might not be obvious to you. We pay attention to every aspect of your business dreams to get you from where you are to where you want to be.

We know that no two paths in entrepreneurship are the same and don't happen in straight lines. They zig, zag, and zoom. Detours, rest stops, and reroutings happen in almost every business. Human nature makes some issues unavoidable, but most problems can be reduced or avoided altogether if we have someone on the outside who has been through the process of creating and building businesses and who can assist us.

Speaking of Detours and Missteps in Business

It's funny how entrepreneurs do not speak about these detours. It has become ingrained in us to smile and say, "Everything is great!" It really does not matter if business is great or not. That is what we say.

After working for others for many years, I started my first business in 2007. It was a luxury interior design service. The first year was fabulous, and I thought (arrogantly) that I had mastered this business thing! I was doing great—until the recession of 2008 brought decline and humility. Do you know what happened to my design business when people could no longer understand the value of investing in my services? It dried up. I had been standing in a beautiful room full of potential and opportunity, with sunlight beaming through the windows and an open door of clients coming through. Then it was as if the door slammed closed, someone turned off the sun, removed the window, and I was standing left in the dark and couldn't find my way out. I wasn't the only business that felt that pain. It was rampant. Yet, I would be in a showroom and run into another interior designer.

"How's business?"

"Oh, great… You?"

"Great!"

It was code for what we were really asking each other, "Are you feeling the pinch, or is it just me?"

Current-Me would like to share that our nation has more than 33.1 million small, unique businesses—do you realize how cool that is? Do you recognize the depth of knowledge that could be shared if we were honest about what happens in business? It blows my mind.

Since forming Your Biz Rules in 2014, I've been on a mission to share the stories of the entrepreneurial journey through our content and speaking on stages around the nation. I want you to realize that even if business feels crazy, that's "normal." Having detours to navigate around is "normal." No matter where you are in your business or what you are trying to create, it is "normal." While some of your actions may have probably contributed to your detours, many are related to the entrepreneurial journey—not whether you are doing something "right." I want to keep sharing the stories—and the strategies to help the "normal" feel less chaotic.

Many of my clients are just like you. When you started your business, you saw a need or problem that needed to be solved and were passionate about it. Perhaps you saw someone else try but knew you could do it better.

You want to do good work and are inspired by the possibility that a successful business can help your family now and in the future. It's about money and creating something that lasts and makes a difference for your loved ones and the mark you want to leave in this world. You're building a future that shows what's important to you and leaves a positive legacy for others to remember.

You dream about being successful, what it could mean, what you could do. After all, no one has ever said, "I'm going to start a business to go broke, be exhausted, and doubt my ability to make a decent income."

Yet that is exactly what does happen. People go into debt for their business. They drain their 401K. They feel like they have failed, which can lead to shame and blame. The truth is, very few people make it big on their first try or without the help and guidance of others—so why do we expect to be able to be an overnight success?

"Timing, perseverance, and ten years of trying will eventually make you look like an overnight success."
—*Biz Stone, Co-Founder of Twitter*

So, who is this book for? According to the Small Business Administration, a small business is defined as a business with less than 500 employees. For many entrepreneurs, that's a pretty big business. Others define a small business as one with less than $5 million in revenue. Micro-businesses typically have less than $1 million in revenue. The good news is that small and micro businesses comprise more than 90 percent of businesses. The strategies and philosophies shared in this book are perfect for you because they are based on good business practices.

This book is perfect for business owners from any industry because business fundamentals are universal. Our clients span 17 industries, including service-only, service-product mix, and product-only businesses. What unites them is a common goal: to grow their businesses profitably and intelligently. No matter your field, you'll find plenty of valuable insights in this book.

My goal for you is to shift how you see your business.

I want to help you grow your business to create one that is profitable, sustainable, and one that you love. I want to talk to you as if we are having a conversation to help your business grow more successfully.

So, let's start this journey together.

Chapter 1

YOUR BUSINESS, YOUR RULES
Navigating the Road to Strategic Success

"The journey of a thousand miles
begins with one step."
—Lao Tzu

Have you ever wished someone could swoop in and "save" your business, making everything easier and more enjoyable? I understand that feeling. While I don't have a magic wand to instantly transform your business, here's the powerful truth: you already possess the ability to turn things around. You are the key to your business's success.

You picked up this book for a reason. You may be a business owner facing challenges that weren't part of your plan. You may be proactive, looking to improve by learning from the experiences of others. Or, your business is doing well, but you have a nagging feeling it could be doing even better.

I'm glad you are looking for a solution to fix whatever is ailing your business or avoid problems that might occur if you were not researching now. By taking this step, you're demonstrating a commitment to your business and your future. You have the strength and the potential to make your business thrive, and I'm here to guide and support you on this transformative journey.

There Are No Quick Fixes

It's a common sentiment: "If only I had the answers to fix my business! Then life would be better. My friend did this one thing, and it totally fixed his business!" Many business owners feel this way when they're frazzled and overwhelmed. But the truth is relying on quick fixes or hoping for a single solution to transform your business won't give you lasting success.

Here's the reality. While getting guidance is beneficial, you must develop your own problem-solving skills. Blending the advice you receive with your actions and decisions is essential. Keeping your vision of your business alive and actively participating in changing your business helps you build a strong business. You can adapt to change and prepare to tackle obstacles head-on. By combining learning from others with your own experiences, you'll gain a better understanding of your business and strengthen your ability to lead it toward success, even when times are tough.

Expecting an instant fix is like believing a fitness tracker will make you fit without any effort. It does not magically fix the situation and only leads to disappointment. The first step toward real growth is understanding that quick solutions don't work in business. I had to learn this the hard way.

In my first business, I lost 50 percent of my revenue almost overnight during a recession because I was in the luxury industry. I entered a dark, depressing period, feeling like a personal failure. Many businesses were struggling, but I took it to heart. I punished myself by working longer, harder hours, stopped paying myself (even though I continued to pay my staff), and embarked on a crusade to save my business. And it almost broke me.

I was relentless. I bought and read countless business books. They offered great insights but didn't save my business. I joined not one but two industry masterminds (a group of peers who meet to give each other advice and support, often led by a facilitator or coach) and attended numerous conferences, searching for the magic answer to turn my business around. I thought if I could do what everyone else who seemed successful was doing, I would find success, too.

Nothing worked. Absolutely NOTHING. Have you had this experience yourself?

Maybe it wasn't the Great Recession or 2020 that rocked your business. Sometimes, unexpected challenges can arise even when the economy is booming, and your business is thriving. It doesn't need to be a worldwide or nationwide event to send your business into a tailspin. It can be a private, personal event as well. Divorce, illness, trauma, and death can have the same impact.

Working tirelessly without seeing any returns can make you feel stuck in a rut, like a hamster endlessly running on a wheel but getting nowhere. But here's the empowering truth: even in these difficult moments, you have the strength and resilience to navigate through. These setbacks are part of the journey that allows you to develop the grit and problem-solving skills needed to overcome them. You are not alone in facing these challenges. Acknowledging your challenges is the first step toward finding solutions and emerging stronger.

Before you think I'm against things like reading to improve your skills or masterminds, I'm all for them. We run a program similar to a mastermind, the Profitable Growth Incubator, which combines the collective strength of a traditional mastermind with the personalized guidance of one-on-one coaching. Books can be a great place to start a journey to brush up on the skills you need to be a better business owner. Conferences are a great source of idea generation and connection with business owners who can help and inspire you to move the needle in your business.

Then why don't all of these resources fix your business? The answer lies in the mind.

The Limiting Impact of an Entrepreneurial Mindset

I was working with a business owner whose business was a couple of years old. She believed in what she did. Truly, she did. Her knowledge of how to help people with various skills blew my mind. She was a master of her craft.

Although she had been in business for a couple of years, her venture was still in its early stages because she needed to establish a dependable method for acquiring clients and generating a steady cash flow. Our primary goal was to refine her marketing and sales strategies. We aimed to establish a reliable system for bringing in clients and cash.

As with every client, we started by reflecting on past successes to understand which strategies were effective and why they worked. We revisited her ideal client profile to ensure we knew exactly who we were targeting. Next, we selected the marketing strategy with the most promise for generating leads. After that, my client took the reins and began implementing these strategies.

We focused on developing appealing service packages and devised a service diagram for her. This visual guide outlined the most probable service a new client might choose first and what they might need next. This way, when potential clients started to show interest, there was a clear plan to guide them to the service they needed.

The work showed promise. The leads started to come in. In the previous six months before working with us, there were only 15 leads. We started with 15 leads in two weeks, a clear indicator that the changes we made were working.

Here's where it gets interesting. As part of our work, we determined the benchmarks for her business based on its performance. These key performance indicators (KPIs) give a baseline for growth. Based on her sales skills and conversion, she should have landed three new clients with those 15 leads. That didn't happen.

I consider that normal and to be expected. After all, the sales conversion rate is the average of times you would expect to receive a sale after a certain number of leads. Inconsistency happens in real life; results don't happen according to averages. We waited for a few more leads to come in to give a chance for results to average out to this baseline. Then, we could see if the leads would start to convert.

No dice. *Interesting.* All the good indicators were there. Yet, the results were not materializing.

We went back into the process. Were we attracting the right client, one who would purchase? It seemed so. How was the sales conversation going? Were the right questions being asked to guide the lead to a yes? How was the service being positioned or offered?

When we role-played the sales conversation, all the elements were there. We adjusted, added a few incentives around the first purchase, and waited to see what would happen.

More and more leads came in, but not a single sale. All in all, there were 100 ideal client leads, yet not a single sale.

Sometimes, fixing the broken parts of a business is a bit like being an experienced mechanic with grease up to your elbows, looking perplexed at a high-performance engine that should be running smoothly but isn't. You've checked and rechecked the components, and everything should work, but it won't turn over.

That is what was happening here. What was the block? It came down to mindset. Our client held a common belief throughout our time together: "No one sees the value in what I do. No one wants to pay for my services. The people in my town are too close-minded to want my services."

Where do these thoughts come from? They are learned over time and can be explained simply: A thought that happens over time becomes a belief. A belief repeated over time becomes a truth. A truth repeated over time becomes a reality.

"Whether you think you can or you think you can't,
you're right."
—Henry Ford

Beliefs like the one in the story above act as barriers to the path and become self-fulfilling prophecies, creating a trap of faulty logic. The truth is that no matter what you are doing, other successful businesses do what you do. If success is eluding you, and you are doing the right things, then it is time to ask the hard question. Is the problem your belief?

What you believe matters. The words you choose matter. What if all you need to do is change your beliefs, the silent thoughts you think that keep you playing smaller than your potential?

Understanding that your mindset can make a difference is why all those conferences, books, and masterminds can not save your business. This was a part of my journey, as much as the business owner in our story.

The roadblock of the mind also explains why I can only be your guide on this part of the journey. There is only one person who can save your business.

YOU.

This is the reason we can't offer any guarantees. Ultimately, I don't have control over what my clients—or you—choose to do or not do, nor can we control what they believe. While there are many reasons why people resist change, they usually come down to a single factor: fear.

We can help you rewrite this self-talk and manage your inner critic's automatic negative thoughts. You only have to choose to do something different and believe that it is possible.

If you learn this lesson, you will open yourself up to the greatest power in your business. You have great power if you can get in the right mindset.

The truth is that you can shift your business. You can make shifts to market to your target audience. Do you have clients who complain and ask for discounts? Shift away from them and find ones happy to work with you. Do you struggle with employees who don't do their job and maybe even steal from the business? Make a shift. Do you need more clients or profit? You can fix that. It may feel uncomfortable, but this book is here to help guide you on the journey. Know that you are not alone on that journey.

When I realized that I had the power to change my first business, I felt an overwhelming urge to cry. It hit me that if I had the power to fix things, it also meant that I had inadvertently created everything I disliked about my business. At first, this realization was disheartening, but then I understood something crucial. If I had the ability to create these problems, I also had the ability to solve them and build my business back better. Up to this point, I felt that everything in my business happened to me. Afterward, I understood that I had more power than I had realized.

I couldn't blame myself for the mistakes I made when I didn't know better in my first business. Instead, I chose to focus on the future and used my newfound awareness to make positive changes. This shift in perspective was empowering—it meant I had the control and the responsibility to shape my business into something I loved and was proud of.

I love the phrase from Uncle Ben in the Spider-Man movie: "With great power comes great responsibility." That became my catchphrase as I set out to repair and redesign my business. For me, it was an empowering motivation to move forward.

I give you the power that I gave myself. If you created it, you can change it. If you take the responsibility for it, you can shift it. Anything becomes a possibility.

When you see a part of your business that isn't working, ask yourself, "What did I do to create the situation?" Do this without blame and with an objective mind. Then, ask yourself, "How can I fix it?"

If you are struggling on the rollercoaster of feast and famine—what are you doing or not doing that creates the situation? What beliefs are contributing to the problem?

Your beliefs, actions, and the emphatic statements you repeatedly say will become self-fulfilling prophecies. Be careful to only speak things into truth that meet your vision.

I would like to add some caution at this point. It's easy to slide into judgment when you become more aware of poor choices and missed opportunities. Please do not go there. The point of this exercise is to find opportunities for change.

The emotion you may feel is real, natural, and human. Experience it. Take a deep breath and let it go with the promise to do better and be better. The slippery slope of shame, blame, and guilt do not serve your best interests.

To tackle business challenges, obstacles, and problems effectively, we need to start with honesty. At the beginning of this book, take a moment to list them. Then, jot down any beliefs or principles you've inadvertently turned into rules within your business.

Don't know what those are? Ask the people closest to you to help you brainstorm reasons why your business may not be as successful as it could be. Listen objectively, like a reporter collecting information and data to write a story. Resist the urge to become defensive. The people closest to you often can see the answers that evade you.

When you've listed all the negative thoughts holding your business back, flip them into positive ones. For instance, if a client thinks that no one appreciates their work or is willing to pay for it, we suggest changing that to: "I can find people who understand my work, see its value, and are happy to pay for it."

Make sure your rephrased thoughts are both believable and attainable. They should bring a smile to your face and fill you with hope. If they don't resonate initially, remember that these positive perspectives are already within you—you wrote them down for a reason.

Recognizing and changing limiting beliefs is the first step toward a healthier business mindset. As you've begun to understand the profound impact your mindset and beliefs have on your business, it's equally crucial to align your daily operations with strategic focus and adaptability. This next section will delve into practical strategies that are essential for maintaining the health and alignment of your business.

Navigating Your Business with Strategic Focus and Adaptability

In business, it's easy to get caught up in the whirlwind of daily tasks and endless strategies, making it challenging to stay focused on what truly matters. The latest trends, the opinions of others can easily blow you and your business off course. Without a strategy to get back on track, it's no wonder that business owners get lost.

To help you master the skill of navigating your business with strategic focus and adaptability, here are three recommendations: stop looking for quick fixes, identify your North Star, and remember that while everything works in business, nothing works universally. We'll now explore each of these concepts and how they can guide you on the path to clarity and success.

Stop Looking For Quick Fixes

Stop chasing shiny objects, stop looking for the one thing that can save your business, stop looking for the magic wand, stop falling for the "traps" that derail your business, and stop looking for the "get rich quick" schemes. As I said previously, there are no quick fixes. It took you a while to get where you are, and it will take a bit to get where you want to be. If you can let go of the "when", you'll realize that you can "win" more frequently.

As you'll see later, we can strategically plan for quick wins, but any change takes time and often happens as a culmination of several efforts. When you shift away from the quick fixes, you become more strategic, which builds momentum and drives better results. We will talk more about these concepts when we dive into growth.

Identifying Your North Star and Aligning Your Business with Core Values

In the night sky, the North Star is the one point around which every other star revolves. It does not move but always stays in place.

In business, the North Star is simply remembering why you are in business—your vision, goals, passions, ideal client, and everything you want to accomplish with your business. If you are considering a shift in your business or something doesn't seem to work for you, develop the discerning muscle to check your North Star with a possible solution to ensure the two are in alignment.

To illustrate this example, let's look at another client who came to work with us after working with another mentor. Only one year before, the client's business was steady, growing with some growth pains. They began working with the mentor to grow their business to be bigger and work with better clients. Unfortunately, the result was the business shrank almost to zero in the year.

Now, it is easy to point fingers at the mentor. One might think that their formula or binder didn't work. It is also easy for a mentor to point fingers at the client, saying they didn't follow the formula or do the work. None of these scenarios were at play.

After understanding my client's goals when she joined the previous mentor's program, exploring her vision for the business and personal life, the values that guide actions, her ideal client, and the preferred work methods that made up her North Star, the root of the issue became apparent.

By trying to follow the formula exactly as her previous mentor wrote it, the client was building a business that was out of alignment with her North Star. The business was headed in a direction her heart didn't want to go. When business decisions conflict with your North Star, your business is divided. Pulling in opposite directions, a business divided goes nowhere.

The solution was to use her North Star to rebuild the business. Our client gained clarity on the new rules of her business and aligned her business to those rules. Business picked up again, the growing pains were manageable, and the owner had a newfound sense of peace and calm about the future.

Completing the "North Star" test on your own business will help you determine which strategies are worth pursuing and which are not. By acting as a compass to keep the business on course, you increase the likelihood of enjoying more of the success you create.

Everything Works, and Nothing Works in Business

The key to staying true to your North Star is understanding that "everything works and nothing works in a business." When something doesn't work, it is all too easy to doubt your North Star and to change course too soon. This concept applies an attitude of experimentation to finding what works best for your business.

The success of business strategies can be highly situational and variable. *"Everything works"* suggests that almost any strategy or method can be effective under the right circumstances. *"Nothing works"* implies that no guaranteed, one-size-fits-all solution always leads to success in every situation. Strategies that work well in one context may fail in another due to different variables. This can be incredibly frustrating. How can you tell if the strategies you are trying need you to stay focused and disciplined or if you're just chasing the impossible?

The goal is to make the changes strategically, not from a reactionary state of mind. Well-rounded, effective decision-making and informed decisions come when you combine intuitive insights and data analysis. Add feedback loops and key performance indicators to let you know if you are on or off track and what to do next. By doing this, you will have great results. This system of managing your business will yield a better answer than guessing. By the end of this book, you will understand these concepts better and be far better prepared to make strategic changes in your business. These are foundations that I wish all business owners knew.

Another thing to consider is that we only advocate changing strategies *after* they have had a chance to bear fruit. You wouldn't plant a peach tree on day one and stamp it out on day 12 because it had not had a chance to bear fruit, would you? It takes a good two to three years for a peach tree to bear fruit. I am not saying you must wait two to three years on a strategy. I am saying that you need to wait long enough for the strategy to work.

We can learn another lesson from peach trees that can help us as we look at being strategic in business. Peach trees need certain conditions to bear fruit—like chilling hours. Chilling hours are the amount of time a variety of peach trees needs to spend at a specific temperature to bear fruit. If you live in an area where you barely get 100 chilling hours a winter and plant a tree that needs 500 chilling hours, you have entered into an exercise in futility. No matter how many trees you plant or how long you wait, that tree will not produce fruit because the conditions will never be in place for the tree. Some strategies fail due to a lack of chilling hours. They will never bear fruit in your business and should be dropped when that is recognized.

This nuanced understanding comes with time and experience, but if a change is warranted, be brave. Be willing to do something different enough to get a different enough result.

I had this epiphany after reading this quote often attributed to Albert

Einstein, "Insanity is doing the same thing over and over and expecting a different result." That was it, I thought to myself, *I was insane.* When the quote settled in my brain, I looked at all the strategies I had implemented in my first business and was shocked to find they were all basically the same. And they all had the same lukewarm result. And I kept investing in them.

When I realized that if I wanted a different result, I needed to invest in strategies, habits, and tasks that were different enough to produce different results. My business only needed to provide me with the information to understand what was working and what was not. By the end of the book, you'll understand where this happens in your business and how to set up a system that keeps you ahead of the game.

These are the lessons that I hope you learn from this book and can put into practice in your business. Imagine having someone in your corner with a wealth of experience who can ask the tough questions, challenge your assumptions, and provide unwavering support when needed most. That's what you'll find in these pages. I'll help you identify and break free from beliefs holding you back and help you define your guiding principles. With a clear direction, you'll develop the intuition to know when to stay the course and when to dare to be different. My goal is for you to achieve the business growth and results you desire to build a more profitable, sustainable, and fulfilling business legacy.

This clarity lays the groundwork for understanding one of your business's most crucial aspects—its finances. In the following chapter, we'll explore the mindset, expectations, habits, and actions that can shape your financial success. By aligning your financial goals with your business vision, you will gain the clarity and confidence needed to establish a sustainable path to profitability.

Chapter 2

MASTER YOUR FINANCES
Beyond Vanity Metrics to Sustainable Profit

"Revenue is vanity, profit is sanity,
and cash is king."
—Unknown

The saying "Revenue is vanity, profit is sanity, and cash is king" is a famous adage in the business world. Nobody's sure who coined this saying, but it's a golden rule that many people have repeated. Here is why I share it today. I'm going to give you the choice between two businesses.

Business A is a $2 million business. Business B is a $750,000 business. Which one would you choose?

I believe I heard several readers say that they would take the $2 million business. But if we dive in a little deeper, will that remain true?

Now, let's say that Business A is a $2 million business and makes $200,000 in profits. Business B, at $750,000, also makes $200,000 in profits. Which would you choose now? Does the decision get harder?

Further investigation reveals that Business A is struggling to pay its bills. It is in debt and needs more money to stay open. Business B, however, has money to cover its bills and has set some aside for the future.

I won't even ask which business you would choose now, as I assume you want a profitable business that is not on the brink of shutting its doors. Isn't it surprising that the $750,000 business is doing better than the $2,000,000 business in this case?

Unfortunately, we see businesses like this all the time, broke million-dollar businesses. They fit into the first part of the statement, "Revenue is vanity." Chasing revenue just for the sake of it is vanity if it creates a cash-poor business. In the quest to become a million-dollar business, we often overlook the role of profits and cash flow.

Profits are sanity because having more money coming in than going out generally offers peace of mind. However, we can't stop there because profits do not equal cash. A business can show profits on its financial statements and still run broke. If you've ever had your CPA present you with a tax bill larger than your bank account balance, you know this statement is true.

That's why understanding cash flow is crucial. Your cash flow gives you the power to operate smoothly, pay your team, and make strategic choices about future investments. It's the power to choose what to invest in next and the fuel to keep going.

Yet they are all related. You must have enough revenue to produce profits and enough profits to produce cash to keep your business healthy and thriving in the long run.

There are many reasons for starting a business, but there is one definition of a successful business:

A successful business produces
more cash than it spends.

Conversely, it's easy to see that a lack of cash will, by definition, cause your business to fail.

The reasons you run out of funds may vary—inefficient operations, poor sales strategies, unexpected expenses—but the result is the same: without sufficient cash flow, your business cannot remain open.

Confronting Your Money Mindset

This leads me to an important question: How do you feel about money? If discussing money, or even raising the topic, makes you uneasy—perhaps causing your stomach to churn, your blood pressure to rise, or making you feel slightly offended—then you might need to address some issues with your money mindset. Many business owners struggle with this, and it significantly impacts your business.

Cultural norms, family values, and personal experiences shape one's beliefs about money. These beliefs drive financial behaviors and decisions, affecting financial success, overall well-being, and satisfaction.

No one is immune. I had to face some money mindset issues when I worked to rebuild my first business. These issues were formed when I was young, and I had to overcome them later in life and shift my thoughts from limiting to expansive to make space for the success I craved.

Growing up, we were poor. We should have been on assistance, but we hovered just over the threshold for it—stuck in no man's land.

My mother worked two jobs from 6 a.m. to midnight, and my father did nothing except spend money we didn't have to spend.

Every day, debt collectors called the house and left messages to scare my parents into action. I heard every message and felt every harsh word in the recordings.

When I was ten years old, one of my responsibilities was planning the weekly menu and grocery shopping. When it was time to go grocery shopping, I loved riding my bike on the main roads for the two miles it took to get to the grocery store. This weekly trip was my little adventure, offering a thrilling sense of freedom and independence as I navigated the neighborhood. I worked hard on those trips, checking the grocery ads and gathering leftover coupons from the neighbors' Sunday paper that they shared with us. Every single penny mattered because I had $20/week to feed my family of five.

We ate a lot of macaroni and cheese, ramen, spaghetti, tuna, and hot dogs. If the sales were in our favor, I could buy a Little Debbie Star Crunch package or Nutty Buddy Bars. *I felt like a champion those days.*

But if the odds weren't in our favor, I would tearfully have to decide what to have the cashier remove from the cart so that I could pay with the cash I had in my pocket, *leaving me feeling defeated.*

These experiences colored my emotions around money. My self-worth got wrapped up in my ability to stretch $20 weekly. The shame I felt with every debt collector's phone call. These emotions would guide my interactions with money for the next 20 years.

I share this story to illustrate that our money experiences create emotional reactions. These money stories get imprinted at such a soul level that we don't always realize they impact our everyday lives.

I had no idea how my money mindset stories colored how I ran my first business until I looked back. It was full of days where I felt like a champion when the money flowed, followed by a deep shame when my bank accounts were low. I never fell behind on my bills, but that was only because I could feel the weight of the fear and shame with the thought that debt collectors might call.

After recovering from the recession of 2008-2009, I was tired of the weight of the worry. I came to a crossroads, realizing that I had to change how I managed and related to money. I couldn't live up to my potential if I carried the baggage of my money stories forward. The mindset issues held me back in devastating ways.

Being successful with your money mindset requires recognizing the negative or limited beliefs and working to transform them into positive and empowering ones that align with your financial goals. Limited mindset beliefs are sneaky and immensely creative. They get us locked into such faulty money stories that hamper our success. Everyone has some story that colors their money management.

For me, I realized that I wasn't managing the money in my business. *It* was managing *me.* I hoped and prayed that it would be there, rejoicing when it was, freaking out when it wasn't. I had a growing distrust of money in my business.

I knew I had to rewrite the story for myself. To do so, I had to redefine what I wanted my relationship with money to be. I needed to stop the automatic negative thoughts that fueled my fear. I had to shift my habits and intentions to have a better relationship with money.

Today, instead of money managing me, I manage it with confidence and purpose. I've rewritten my financial story from scarcity to mindful abundance, ensuring that my decisions are driven by optimism and strategic foresight. This transformation has alleviated the emotional burden and opened doors to new opportunities for growth and stability in my personal life and business.

Through this book, our goal is to guide you on a similar path, helping you identify and reshape your money mindset so that you, too, can move forward with financial confidence and success.

Take a minute and consider your first memory of hearing others talk about money. What was said at that time? Where do you have strong emotional responses to money? How does this memory and the money story around it affect you today?

Dodging Disasters: Five Common Money Traps to Avoid as an Entrepreneur

Our stories play out in many ways in your business, and we see five common money traps that these stories create. They are:

1. Find Your Passion, and the Money Will Follow
2. Skipping the Math
3. Hard Work Gets Rewarded
4. Hope and Prayer, or Wait and See
5. Growth Solves Cash Problems

Let's look at each of these traps closely to understand the trap and how to navigate around it.

Money Trap #1: Find Your Passion and the Money Will Follow

"Find your passion" for a business makes for a great inspirational photo for your wall or meme for your social media, but it is only half of the story.

We believe you should find your passion. Passion is important. It is the reason you do what you do. Passion will help you through some tough times. It can motivate you like nothing else. It can drive you to find the solution and experiment to find your secret sauce.

The second half of the phrase, "and the Money Will Follow," does not necessarily happen. Passion just won't pay the bills.

Not all passions are profitable. Some passions are better suited to the nonprofit arena, yet even nonprofits must produce profits to reinvest in the cause and have an impact.

No matter how enthusiastic you are, if there's no market demand or people aren't willing to pay for your offering, it won't translate into a sustainable business model.

Interestingly, these three components—what you are passionate about, the problems you solve, and finding people willing to pay for solutions—perfectly define an ideal client. A powerful tool to help you understand your business better.

If you find yourself caught in this money trap, a helpful step is to evaluate your passion critically. Ask yourself: Does my passion align with a genuine need? Is there a problem that I can solve that people are willing to pay for? This approach helps you identify if there's a real market for what you're passionate about.

This trap is closely related to the misleading belief of "If You Build It, They Will Buy It." While popularized by the movie *Field of Dreams*, this trap doesn't have a movie ending. It still focuses on what the business owner is passionate about, often overlooking what the potential customers need and want.

Both of these slogans have a problem of market alignment, which is just a polite way of saying nobody wants what you're selling. The real danger of this trap is that it can take years for a business owner to realize they're stuck in it. It's much wiser to test your business concept with potential customers early on to see if there's a genuine need, desire, and willingness to pay.

We have business owners run ideas past us occasionally and test them to see if they might fall into this trap. In one case, a close friend once asked for feedback on an idea to offer tech support to senior citizens to help them use email and social media. He envisioned having office hours in senior centers and charging an affordable rate for 15 to 30 minutes of help.

We began by asking a few questions about the business model, such as how the business would deliver and create value for its clients. We continued with a few critical questions we think every business owner should be able to answer:

- What problem are you trying to solve?
- Is this problem widespread and compelling?
- What is the "pain" or consequences for your potential clients if this problem isn't solved?
- Are your ideal clients prepared to pay for a solution?

By this point of the discussion, my friend felt confident that he had affirmative answers to these questions. However, the next question brought up the next money trap.

I asked him, "What does success in this business look like to you?" He replied that success would mean the ability to leave a full-time job and be in control of his own destiny. This leads us to our second money trap. It was time to do the math and see if that was possible.

Money Trap #2: Skipping the Math

If we are honest, only a small percentage of the population loves math. Other people avoid it at any cost. The truth is that a successful business relies on solid math. For your business to thrive, the numbers need to add up. If the math of the business doesn't work, then the business won't work either.

Our friend in the story above skipped the math. With a few more questions about income expectations, resources, overhead, and planned pricing, it became clear the business model would not achieve the desired result. Sure, it could bring in a little spending money, but it would not replace a full-time salary. It just wasn't scalable.

Scalable business models are part of the success formula. We will explore this topic later in the book when discussing business models and pricing for profit.

For now, I want to make the following point: When building your business, "start with the end in mind." This phrase, attributed to Stephen Covey in *The 7 Habits of Highly Effective People*, emphasizes the power of a clear vision to guide actions and decisions. Then, do the math until you've landed on the right business model to help you meet all your goals.

Don't start with the revenue or price, and try to force the math. By beginning with the end in mind, you'll spot when the math stops working on an otherwise viable business idea. But what if you don't do the math beforehand?

We spoke with a sports coach who used to be a trainer at a country club. When he left to start his own business, he initially set his pricing at the same rates the country club had charged.

A year or two later, the owner was struggling to get the business to a level to sustain a personal income. Curious about his goals, I asked him, "How much do you want to earn right now?"

His response? "$10,000 a month."

"Great," I say and ask a few questions. "How do you currently serve your clients? How much do you charge?"

"Well, I'll tell you, but I'm not going to raise my prices," he responded immediately.

Oh, interesting. When we hit a nerve like this, we know a money mindset issue is at play.

"Ok," I say. "How much do you charge?"

"$45 for a 45-minute session. That's what the country club paid me, so that's what I charge because my clients expect that from my industry."

"Well, let me ask you this: How many lessons will you need to give to earn $10,000 monthly?"

Silence. I did the math. The answer is 222.22.

That breaks down to about 11 sessions each day if you only worked weekdays, but you would be working at least 12-13 hours each day. If you wanted a more reasonable day length—if you worked every day of the month, EVERY DAY—you would have to give eight lessons a day at that price.

Even if you manage to maintain your energy for such a rigorous schedule, it's unlikely that one country club could accommodate all those sessions. He would likely need access to several clubs or expand your team to include more trainers to meet his targets realistically.

However, we must still address the pricing strategy, as it remains critical in making your business model sustainable. The math simply does not work as proposed. There is a system for finding the sweet spot of pricing, one that attracts the right client who is thrilled to pay. We'll cover this as well in the book, but know that it may challenge your business model premise to align the business with your personal goals.

Money Trap #3: Hard Work Gets Rewarded

There's a common belief in our society that sacrifice and hard work naturally lead to rewards. Unfortunately, it's not always that straightforward. Many hardworking and deserving people still find themselves living paycheck to paycheck.

This myth assumes you won't be rewarded if you don't work hard. So, the logic follows that if you aren't seeing the rewards and financial gains in your business, you just aren't working hard enough. While there are cases where increased effort may yield results, more often, the issue lies deeper. If you're doing all that needs to be done and still not seeing financial returns, something is wrong at the foundational level that needs fixing.

The key is balancing hard work with smart work. Implementing frameworks that build in ease is crucial. The most profitable businesses are often simple and efficient, free of bottlenecks. They focus on optimizing processes and ensuring every effort contributes effectively to the bottom line. This means evaluating your business operations regularly to identify and eliminate inefficiencies.

One critical mindset shift is moving from viewing profits as a mere reward for hard work to setting intentional goals and creating systems supporting those goals. This involves strategic planning, understanding your market, and continually adapting to changes.

Money Trap #4: Managing Your Money on a Hope and Prayer

Many business owners delay acting when their company's finances slip, effectively managing their money "on a hope and prayer," otherwise known as the "wait and see" method.

This delay can be due to uncertainty about what steps to take, not knowing where to find reliable help, or being paralyzed by shame and guilt. Of all the instinctive reactions—fight, flight, or freeze—many business owners unfortunately freeze.

The insidious nature of this passive approach often catches business owners off guard. It is best personified by the familiar question: How do you boil a frog without it jumping out? The answer is to turn up the heat slowly. The minor changes are harder to feel and do not cause alarm. Depending on your money manager personality (discussed more in the next chapter), you won't notice the decline until it is significant—like the water is boiling.

It's incredibly frustrating to watch clients fall into this trap, knowing that earlier action could have greatly simplified their recovery. Relying on hope or a wait-and-see attitude amounts to indecision, which can be fatal for your business.

Our first step with new clients is to evaluate their cash flow and profitability. Imagine your business as a bucket filled with holes. If you pour water into this bucket, how much water leaks (or revenue)? You could keep pouring more water to compensate, but then you'd lose 30 percent of your profit to leaks. Our approach focuses on patching these leaks, allowing your business to thrive with less overall input and to retain more revenue when we boost your income further. This means you can work less and achieve more.

After evaluating your cash flow and profitability, we install easy-to-maintain cash-flow management tools that provide real-time insights into your financial health. These tools empower our strategists to collaborate with you, identifying and addressing declines proactively. This system offers a window into your business's financial future, enabling you to make informed decisions in minutes, not months.

Whenever possible, avoid this trap of indecision because of its costs. While it might feel safe to wait and see, it is riddled with risks.

Why risk? Most business issues are solvable, but the sooner they're tackled, the less impact they have. Remember, a problem that festers quietly for three months can take another three to resolve. Sure, you could focus on treating the symptoms faster, but it will become a constant battle. Save yourself the stress—address the problem and let all the symptoms disappear.

Money Trap #5: If I Grow, I Will Solve My Cash Problems

Growth is a natural and exciting phase of entrepreneurship. It starts initially when you gain your first clients, expand your client base, and successfully deliver your products or services. It is vital and necessary to grow your business.

When business owners face a cash crunch, they often seek growth. However, your available cash tends to dwindle during rapid growth periods—the classic business oxymoron.

At this stage, you feel caught between a rock and a hard place, thinking the only way forward is to work longer and harder. Yet, that's a limited strategy as well. Despite all your efforts, you'll find yourself burning out, running out of energy and hours in the day.

Here is why this happens: Growth does not produce cash; Growth devours cash. This little cash truth is why one of my first steps with new clients is NOT about *growth* but managing *cash* effectively.

"We were always focused on our profit and
loss statement. But cash flow was not a regularly
discussed topic. It was as if we were driving along,
watching only the speedometer, when in fact,
we were running out of cash."
—Michael Dell, Founder & CEO, Dell Technologies

Consider this: You decide to hire three new employees, which means you'll need new computers, software licenses, desks, chairs, and more. Even if you operate virtually, there are costs for additional email addresses, licenses for platforms like Zoom, Teams, or Google, and access to various programs. All these expenses add up quickly and are necessary to support your expansion.

Once these employees start, they go through onboarding, and by the third month, they might be working independently. But are they fully productive yet? Probably not—and that's normal unless their roles are highly routine and process-driven. You might see a noticeable increase in productivity around the sixth month and gradual improvements every three months over the next year. We typically advise clients not to expect employees to reach peak productivity for about nine months. It takes that long for them to fully learn their roles, understand the team dynamics, and build confidence.

So, at the nine-month mark, can you expect a full return on your investment in these new hires? Not quite. You're just starting to see the returns on your investment. That means you've been investing in these employees for six to nine months before they begin to generate more cash than they cost. Growth Devours Cash.

Based on the *Harvard Business Review* article "A Small Business Is

Not a Little Big Business," the chart "The Truth about Cash & Growth" illustrates this phenomenon.

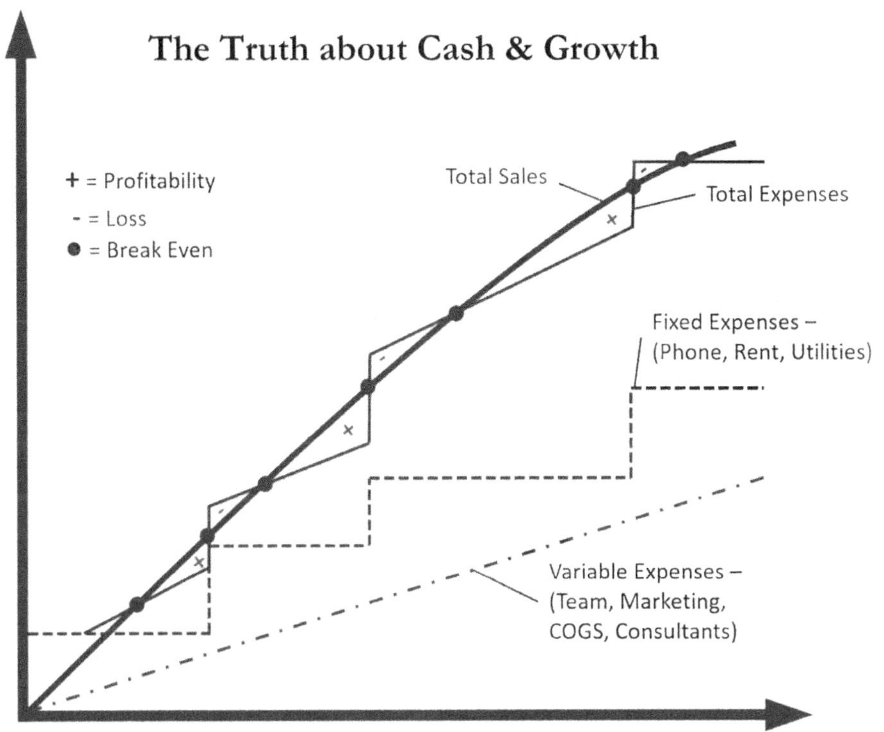

Adapted from *Harvard Business Review*
—A Small Business Is Not a Little Big Business

In business, growth investments tend to happen in stair steps; they shoot up, pushing the business into periods of loss. Then, as the growth investment begins to produce a return, the business experiences profit, and then the business owner chooses more growth, which pushes the business into loss.

These choices have unintended consequences that amplify the feeling of feast or famine.

By their very nature, growth in most businesses *involves an increase in cost.* Understanding this concept is crucial for changing the nature of your cash flow.

Growth is a necessary and normal part of the journey, yet it can drain a business of resources. The answer to getting off this rollercoaster goes back to the ideas in our agrarian history of building up resources during the profitable periods (the summer) to have the resources of money and time that allow growth to mature (the winter).

Understanding that growth alone won't solve your cash problems is crucial for any business owner. As we've explored, managing cash flow effectively and strategically planning your growth is needed to ensure your business remains financially healthy.

Now that we've uncovered some common money traps, let's discuss the three fundamental truths of money behavior. These truths provide a solid foundation for making informed financial decisions and building a resilient business.

The Three Fundamental Truths of Money Behavior

Three behaviors related to money in a business are so common that we call them truths. Understanding these three fundamental truths about money behavior in business is crucial for creating a financially healthy and sustainable enterprise.

Truth #1: Money likes to flow and grow.

Money in business is like a river, constantly flowing and changing course. Whether it's a positive flow like profit draws or employee bonuses or a negative one like mounting debt, money left untended won't magically align with your business or personal goals.

To harness its power, you must be an active steward, guiding its flow with intention and strategy. This proactive approach cultivates a "rich" mindset, ensuring your business thrives amidst the ever-changing currents of finance.

The value of a tool, like a profit plan, is that you can give purpose to profit. With purpose, we can harness this money truth to your benefit.

Truth #2: Simplicity can lead to profitability.

Keeping your financial strategies and operations straightforward can often result in better financial outcomes. When you avoid overly complex systems and focus on clear, efficient processes, you can reduce costs, minimize errors, and make tracking and managing your finances easier.

This streamlined approach can help your business become more profitable by making it easier to see where your money is going and where you can make improvements.

However, every business faces a challenging phase where this does not always hold true—the growth phase. This involves laying solid foundations, and initially, you might find that every dollar you invest in your business only generates about a dollar in revenue. While this stage is crucial, it's typically not very profitable.

The real game-changer is scaling. At the scaling stage, the same dollar invested not only recovers its value but starts multiplying, allowing for significant increases in revenue and profits without the need to work more hours or expand your resources.

Therefore, the intent is to think and plan for your business through stages of growth and scalability, to keep things simple, and to allow profitability to build in the business.

Truth #3: Profits are an intention, not a reward.

The third truth about money is that profits are an intention, not a reward. It's important to ask yourself: What are my profit expectations? When do you expect to become genuinely profitable? What's your magic number?

Treating profit as something that will come later ensures it remains out of reach. From the start, we advocate a paradigm shift: view profits as a primary objective. The goal is to achieve profitability at the lowest possible revenue point. This ensures that profits are not a fleeting hope but a consistent reality.

This is where your choice of revenue model becomes crucial. Revenue models can vary widely in how and when they generate profits. Selecting a model that aligns well with your goals makes a difference. Remember, you can always switch strategies if your current one isn't profitable.

By understanding these five common money traps, you can avoid pitfalls that often entangle business owners. Recognizing these traps gives you the clarity and awareness to manage your finances more strategically and build a foundation that supports sustainable growth. As you continue your entrepreneurial journey, regularly assess your beliefs about money, align your passion with real market needs, and establish a pricing strategy that reflects both your values and goals. By doing so, you'll develop a resilient business that thrives on well-informed financial decisions rather than hopeful assumptions.

Throughout the upcoming chapters on cash flow and pricing, reflect on your reactions and the stories that arise for you. Maybe you've heard echoes of advice like "You need to spend money to make money" or have felt the pull of undervaluing your work due to self-doubt. As we unpack the strategies behind cash flow management and appropriate pricing, these reflections will help you better understand the traps that have impacted your financial health.

Chapter 3

PREDICTABLE PROFITS
Cash Flow Systems That Work

"Money is only a tool.
It will take you wherever you wish,
but it will not replace you as the driver."
—Ayn Rand

If the thought of managing cash flow makes you uneasy or leaves you guessing, you're not alone. Many business owners grapple with the uncertainty and anxiety of not having a firm grip on their finances. But what if you could move forward with unwavering confidence, knowing exactly where your money is and where it needs to go? This chapter is about shifting from fear and confusion to clarity and control.

We'll help you understand your unique money-management archetype, pinpointing your current position and the habits driving your cash flow. By the end, you'll have a system that lets you keep more of what you earn, reduce your financial stress, and empower yourself to build a more stable and secure business. It's not just about the numbers; it's about gaining peace of mind so you can focus on leading your company forward with certainty.

Mastering Money Management and Transforming
Financial Surprises into Strategic Success

When I was running my first business, the recession of 2008 caught me completely by surprise. But that wasn't the only thing that surprised me back then. Getting a client would be a complete surprise to me. Losing a client would be a surprise, too. No money in my bank account would surprise me. I just was not thinking strategically about that business.

I remember getting one of those dream projects with ideal clients and budgets. The profit expected on that short job was $20,000. I remember thinking about what to do with that money in my business. I'd pay down a little debt, buy a new computer, or invest in more marketing.

Six months later, when the final check was deposited, I sat down to look at the money in my bank account. I was proud of our job and wanted to see the proof of it in my bank account.

I logged in, looked at my bank account, and thought—surely this can't be right. Where did it go?

I balanced the account, and sure enough, the balance was correct. I didn't know whether to cry or throw my calculator across the room.

The money wasn't there. It had been spent. I had not even realized I had spent it.

I was shocked. I didn't understand what had happened. The moment was a memorable disappointment in business. It made me realize I was missing the business foundations for managing my cash flow.

I hired a bookkeeper and a CPA, and while I received financial statements every month, cash flow problems persisted.

As my story continued, I was searching for someone or something that could bring my business back after the recession. In search of answers, I went to a conference.

I sat in a fancy ballroom near Union Station in New York City. The ballroom was full of interior designers from all over the country, some very successful, some who had graced magazine covers, and some who, like me, were looking just to cover our bills.

I had no business going on that trip. I had no business paying for the hotel, food, or the ticket price—but I was holding out the hope that this could fix what wasn't working in my business.

In the midst of it, I took a call from our printer. We had just designed a new logo because we were still searching for a way to find new clients (in case you're wondering—a new logo is not the way to attract new clients). The printer called me to get approval for $350 for new stationery, business cards, and envelopes. Can I let you know that it was 2011? Who needed stationery? I was desperate and grasping at straws.

I approved the charge. Then, I checked my bank account. I started to hyperventilate. The room began to spin. It took every fiber of strength not to completely break down in the middle of the ballroom.

My bank account balance was $121. I had just approved $350 for the printer.

I had payroll due in one week. I had just committed myself to new stationery. There were no invoices to collect, no new clients on the horizon, and I had no idea how I was going to make things work.

I felt like an utter and complete failure. I knew I was smart, but it was obvious that I was missing something. Everyone else seemed to be making it—just not me.

I sucked at managing money in my business.

When I thought about it, everything with money was a surprise. I spent my time putting out financial fires right and left, juggling money borrowing from one place to pay for another. You get the picture.

This was my wake-up call. I decided then and there to find a better way. Has that ever happened to you? We know from our work that this is not a unique situation. From our experience, struggling with money management is a common challenge—it doesn't single anyone out. This issue cuts across all businesses, regardless of their size, age, or stage of development.

Part of the solution forward is recognizing where you are and adopting a system to help you work through it. The method we advocate for our clients changes businesses and changes lives.

Our clients may come to us with building debt, unexpected tax bills, and struggling to make payroll. Typically, within one year or less of working together, we have transformed the business into a financially secure one that rewards the owner generously and allows our clients to make investments without worry.

Which is Your Money Management Archetype?

One of the best ways to become the money manager your business needs is to understand your default money management archetype. There are three main ways entrepreneurs manage their money. They are:

- The Ostrich Archetype
- The Rhinoceros Archetype
- The Owl Archetype

The first two archetypes are where most entrepreneurs start. Our goal is to move as many of you as possible into the Owl Archetype.

The OSTRICH Money Archetype

The Ostrich is personified by two actions: burrowing their head in the sand or running away. For the entrepreneur, this would look like avoiding your numbers, never looking at your financials, or simply running from the money in the business.

The Ostrich is an entrepreneur who would rather not know. Usually, this is because there is a fear of knowing where they are. As long as there is plausible deniability, they don't have to take responsibility or action. The problem is you can only take this so far. You can only hide for so long before the little problems in your business become big problems in your business.

The Ostrich—the person who would prefer not to know, often feels that they are too busy to deal with the money or that they are no good at numbers, math, or accounting. This is the person who is surprised by everything in their business. If you can't tell me what your sales have been so far this year off the top of your head, you are probably here. If you have invoices clients have not paid in months, you are probably here.

The Ostrich may have someone else looking at the money for them. They feel safe because they have someone they trust looking at the numbers. This could be a spouse, good friend, or trusted advisor, but it is not you.

The default management style is abdication, and it is risky. No matter how much you may trust a person, it will cost you if you aren't actively involved in managing your business.

We strongly believe that every business owner should have a CPA and bookkeeper to assist with financials. However, it's crucial not to abdicate your participation in financial management. When you step back entirely, the likelihood of issues arising increases significantly. This can result in money being spent in ways you wouldn't approve of or misclassification of expenses. At its worst, this can lead to embezzlement and misappropriation of funds. Poor financial management can cause you to pay more in taxes, incur unnecessary debt, or fall behind on payments. As the owner, you are personally responsible and liable for these situations, making your active participation and advocacy essential.

I recently witnessed a stark example of this at a networking event when a fellow entrepreneur shared their ordeal. They discovered that the person hired to manage their finances had accumulated $300,000 in business debt that the owner had no idea about. The owner had to scramble to come up with the money, lay off staff, and work harder, ultimately leading to burnout as they tried to dig their way out of debt. Unfortunately, this scenario isn't as rare as one might hope. My family experienced something similar when my parents ran a small business. Their accountant embezzled the sales tax money, forcing them to shut down the business and file for bankruptcy.

These experiences underscore the importance of staying engaged with your business's financial health. By actively participating and ensuring your financial team aligns with your goals and values, you can protect your business and foster a stable, prosperous future.

When collaborating with clients who demonstrate this money archetype, we focus on education, empowerment, and addressing money mindset issues. Our approach involves installing strategic systems that build confidence in financial management. By working together, clients who may have previously felt unsure about their financial capabilities gain the knowledge and tools they need to become confident money managers.

The RHINOCEROS Money Archetype

The Rhinoceros is considered one of the world's most dangerous animals. Unprovoked, they seem gentle enough. When threatened, they come charging like a freight train. Rhinos are also known for having limited vision, which means they can easily be triggered by what they can not see.

The Rhinoceros is the entrepreneur who has a little bit of knowledge about the numbers in the business but has a poor vision of what they mean and what to do with them. As such, the littlest things can startle this archetype and send it charging off from one emergency to the next.

The charging never seems to stop, as emergencies and problematic situations keep popping up, sending the business owner rushing from client to client and desperately trying to bring in more money. This is exhausting. The Rhinoceros never feels safe and always feels a sense of impending doom. It sometimes wonders if it might be better off as an Ostrich.

Whether you find yourself responding to money like the Ostrich or the Rhinoceros, these archetypes are full of constant worry and an emotionally draining place to be.

The OWL Money Archetype

The Owl is known for its sight, even in poor or dark situations. Its anatomy allows the Owl to see things from different angles, and its flexibility allows it a whopping 270-degree view.

The Owl knows its numbers and what is going on with its business. This knowledge means it can plan, see any shortfalls months before they come, and take action. Its sight is clear because it can turn its head in one direction to see what the past held and then turn to see where the future is headed, knowing it is in control of the situation.

Cash crunches and cash imperatives don't happen, or at least not as often or drastically. As soon as the Owl sees the potential for one, they are all over it—quick, decisive, and wise.

There are no cash flow surprises as an Owl because you manage your money for today and the future. You have a predictive cash flow report by the month or even day that allows you to see the highs and dips. By seeing your cash flow out by 6 or 12 months, you can foresee emergencies and navigate around them. If you need to invest in an area of your business, you can see the impact on your business before you commit. If you want to disaster- or recession-proof your business, this is where you want to be.

What is the value of this in your business? It is simply everything; it provides choices. Choices are freedom. In late 2019, about two years after implementing cash-management changes into Your Biz Rules, I could pay for all 2020 expenses in advance.

Until then, I paid most of the company expenses monthly. This move positioned me to switch to annual, saving me 10 to 20 percent in expenses. I hadn't foreseen what a gift this would be for the year 2020. Imagine navigating that time when the entire world was shut down for COVID-19 without worrying about your cash flow. This is the strength and security we wish for you. My story isn't the only success story. We've seen clients who adopt our system reap benefits in their business and personally. This is the place where you can put money aside for retirement, pay for college educations, and buy or payoff your home.

Which archetype are you? If you are not the owl, it is time to learn how to become wise like one.

Understanding Your Business Cash Flow

Believe it or not, I estimate that an astounding 80 percent of business failures are due to one core issue: insufficient cash flow. This isn't just a minor setback—it's a widespread problem that can shake the very foundation of your business. However, by understanding and effectively managing your cash flow, you can avoid this pitfall and set your business on a path to stability and long-term success.

Think of cash flow as the fuel that keeps your business engine running. Yet, mastering its management can be tricky. Early in a business, it is common to use personal finance habits, which might not fully translate to business finance. This mismatch can lead to crucial details getting lost in translation, and we may not grasp how cash flow works or the impact of short-term savings on long-term stability.

The reality of the situation is best illustrated with this statistic. The average small business is estimated to have 7 to 21 days of cash on hand, according to *Harvard Business Review* and McKinsey & Co. That's only one to three weeks.

In the upcoming chapters, we will examine some essential financial indicators. Don't worry; it involves basic calculations that you're completely capable of handling. You're well-prepared if you've ever balanced a checkbook or planned a budget. If you want to grab a calculator, feel free. We will start with some easy calculations to examine cash on hand, reserves, and other numbers that will make meaningful improvements in your business.

What is Your Burn Rate/Cash on Hand?

Your burn rate is how much you "burn" or spend daily. Having enough cash on hand in your business means you can easily cover daily expenses and unexpected costs. Without enough cash, even the most profitable business can face operational hiccups that disrupt its ability to function smoothly.

Cash on hand is money to cover your operational expenses such as payroll, rent, utilities, and supplies. It also includes financial reserves to address issues, seek opportunities, reduce your reliance on debt, and make you more creditworthy.

Essentially, it's about being prepared and flexible so you can make the best decisions for your business without stress. Do you have an average of 7-21 days of cash on hand, or do you have more? If you do not know your cash on hand, let's calculate it.

You'll need a Profit & Loss (P&L) Statement, preferably from the last year. On the P&L, find your total expenses. (You can also get this amount from your business taxes.)

Take your total expenses and divide by 260 if your business operates on weekdays only. Divide it by 365 if your business is open every day of the year. If your situation is different, simply multiply the days per week by 52, the number of days in a year.

The result is how much cash your business averages in expenses per day.

Total Expenses ÷ Operational Days = Burn Rate

For instance, if your total expenses were $235,000 and you operated Monday through Friday, here would be the equation:

$$\$235,000 \div 260\ days = \$903.85$$

If this were your business, you would use or "burn" $903.85/day. Now, take a look at your business bank account balance to figure out how much cash on hand is available.

$$\textbf{\textit{Bank Account Balance} \div \textit{Burn Rate} = \textit{Cash on Hand}}$$

Our fictional business has a bank account balance of $16,500. With that information, we would divide our balance by the daily burn rate. Which would look like this:

$$\$16,500 \div \$903.85 = 18.26\ days$$

This would mean that this business had just more than 18 days' worth of cash on hand.

Let's stop for a moment. As you look at your own amount of cash on hand, are you doing a happy dance, or are you feeling let down? Feeling some emotion happens, especially when you get to know your business's money intimately. For now, choose to look at this number as objectively as possible.

Only 10 percent of our clients have the right amount of money on hand when they first come to us. Even those with enough on hand do not feel secure because they are uncertain about what could happen. You'll always worry without the tools and systems to manage cash with confidence. By the close of this chapter, you'll know what these systems are and how they can bring value to your business.

Another important realization to experience is that you have been operating at this level of cash for longer than you realized. It has been a source of tremendous stress. If you've ever worried about making payroll and when it comes time to pay your team, the money is there, then you are knee-deep in this situation. The process we will share with you is the path out of this stressful situation.

How to Establish Reserves in Your Business

The process begins with establishing what you need for reserves. Reserves are the money you set aside for a rainy-day fund for your business. This money is a safety net for the business. If your business is cyclical with moments of feast and famine, the reserves help normalize those swings in your business.

Generally, we recommend three to six months of reserves, yet every business needs something different. In one case, after a careful review of several factors, we recommended nine months of reserves for a company based on how long it took people to pay them. For your business, we would carefully analyze how many months would be needed to give you an accurate forecast of your reserves.

To find how much money we need to save as reserves, multiply the daily expense burn rate we just calculated by the number of days you want to hold in reserves.

$$\textbf{\textit{Burn Rate (\$) x Days of Reserves Needed = Reserves (\$)}}$$

For our purposes today, since we need between three months (90 days) and six months (180 days) of reserves, let's use the value right in the middle with four and a half months (or 135 days).

$$\textbf{\textit{\$903.85 x 135 days = \$122,019.75}}$$

That means our fictional business should have $122,020 "on hand" or bookmarked in the bank for reserves. Imagine for yourself that you have four and a half months of operating cash in the bank. What would improve? How would you feel? And more importantly, how differently would you show up as the owner? This is truly only of the cornerstones of financial stability in your business.

During the process of building reserves which could take a few years to build, there's one affect that you should prepare for in your business. When you build reserves, you build them from profits. Profits generate taxes that will need to be paid. We consider taxes a privilege of profits, but growing profits goes against the grain of other financial advice.

Have you ever heard that by the end of the year, you should spend all the business profits on business expenses and not have to pay taxes on it? I know I have heard it plenty of times.

The problem often lies not in the strategy itself but in its timing. Constantly draining your business of profits leaves you vulnerable, just one disaster away from closing. What's particularly concerning is that the disaster doesn't need to be significant. It could be as simple as being out of the business for three months due to illness, a family emergency, or other personal issues. This happens more often than you might think, and without a financial safety net, your business is in constant danger.

Building up reserves takes time and deliberate effort. It might take a year or more to reach your financial goals. While you can accelerate this process, it typically requires temporarily cutting back on other expenditures.

Establishing a sustainable cash flow system is crucial for consistently supporting all parts of your business. When you build these reserves, they come from your profits. Remember, profit is the privilege of paying taxes. Embrace it and celebrate it. The higher your tax bill, the more money you've made. As we discuss setting up cash flow management systems, we'll cover how to plan for taxes effectively. I also recommend working with a tax-planning specialist to help mitigate your tax liabilities.

As your business grows, keep in mind that the amount of reserves you need will also grow. So, set aside time to review and readjust your reserves regularly throughout the year.

The good news is that once your reserve is built, you can enlist your financial planner or small business banker to put the money to work by earning interest. A certain amount of money should always be liquid and able to be used within days. However, the need to dip into the reserves will be minimized monthly with strategic systems in place.

Now that we understand our cash-flow situation, it is time to manage your finances successfully.

The Essential Cash-Flow Tools for Business Success

You need tools and information to help you manage your business. We are going to discuss the elements that offer a robust cash-flow management system, each offering a slightly different perspective. You need your financial statements, a budget, a profit plan, and a predictive cash-flow tool.

Let's start by looking at your financial statements. As the owner, you should always have direct and immediate access to your finances. Why? Well, you are ultimately responsible for them. To effectively manage them, you should be able to access the right report in minutes, not days.

These reports should be coming to you monthly, preferably by mid-month. Reviewing January's reports in April does little to help you monitor your business's health.

If you don't understand your financial statements, then get your bookkeeper or CPA to sit down and explain the implications to you so that you do. Or, find firms like ours that offer Fractional CFO services as part of our business advisory services. Your financial partners should be patient and help you understand what the numbers are saying and the strategies that need to be implemented. Understanding your numbers helps turn those numbers into strategies.

Your financial statements comprise three main reports, which we will discuss next. Each report is a "snapshot" of a period that combines to tell your business's past and present story and can be used to predict its future story.

Profit and Loss Statement (P&L)

Think of the Profit and Loss statement as a detailed report card that shows how well your business has performed over a certain period—like a month, quarter, or year. It lists all your revenues (what you've earned from selling products or services) and your expenses (what it costs to run your business, including materials, salaries, and rent).

The bottom line of this statement tells you if you made a profit (earned more than you spent) or took a loss (spent more than you earned). It's like looking at the outcome of a recipe—did the ingredients (expenses) you put in turn out a delightful dish (profit), or was something off that needs adjustment?

Balance Sheet

The Balance Sheet is a snapshot of your business's financial health at a specific moment in time, most often a day. It shows what your business owns (assets), what it owes (liabilities), and what's left over for you as the owner (equity). Here's a simple way to think about it:

Assets: These are things you own that have value, like cash, inventory, equipment, and property.

Liabilities: These are your debts and obligations, like loans, credit card balances, and bills you must pay.

Equity: This is your stake in the business after all liabilities are subtracted from assets. It includes your initial investment, any retained earnings, and so on.

The Balance Sheet is like you're taking a photo of everything your business owns and owes. The balance sheet helps you understand if your overall business structure is sturdy (more assets than liabilities) or if it's leaning too heavily on debts.

Cash Flow Statement

The Cash Flow Statement tracks the actual cash coming in and going out of your business over a specific period, often a month, quarter, or year. Unlike the P&L, which can include non-cash items like depreciation, the Cash Flow statement gives you a real-time look at your business's liquidity. It's broken into three parts:

1. **Operating Activities:** This includes cash received from customers and cash paid for day-to-day expenses.

2. **Investing Activities:** This covers cash used for, or generated from, buying or selling assets, like purchasing equipment or selling an old vehicle.

3. **Financing Activities:** This section shows cash exchanges involving fundraising or repayments, such as taking out a loan, repaying it, or issuing stock.

You can think of it as monitoring the water levels in three tanks: operating, investing, and financing. Each flow contributes to your business's overall cash pool. You should understand whether you have enough liquid cash to cover immediate needs, like paying suppliers or employees.

Combining these three reports provides a comprehensive view of your business's financial health. They show how much you might be earning or spending and how those earnings and spending affect your overall assets, liabilities, and cash position. It's like knowing the score, checking the health, and monitoring the stamina of your business all at once!

These statements are, however, about the past. We review these monthly with our clients to stay in tune with the business performance. We also compare how these reports change for the same time period year over year.

Many business owners eventually stop closely examining their financial statements. This oversight can lead to missing crucial insights for effectively managing their business's cash flow. We do not recommend this. We use these statements and two more elements to provide a well-rounded view of the cash flow.

Create a Budget

While not considered part of your financial statements, there is another step you can take to turn them into a power-management tool. You accomplish this with an annual budget. The budget is compiled using the same structure as your Profit and Loss statement to plan how much money should be spent in each category every month.

Depending on your accounting software subscription, this potentially can be fed back into the system and added as a view of your monthly reports. For our clients who do not have this functionality in their accounting systems, we often bring this information in our monthly CFO reports.

If the financial statements are about the past, the budget is a high-level look at the future. This tool can set sales goals, map out future investments and to a extent, project what the business performance will look like throughout the year.

We based our budget on past performance, a growth forecast, and conversations with our clients to ensure that all bases are covered and the resulting budget is comprehensive.

Integrating a Profit Plan

The next tool is a profit plan. The profit plan puts purpose to where the money will flow when there's a profit. It is where we keep tabs on our growing reserves and funding growth plans. While it might be new to you, a profit plan is based on an older wisdom you may be familiar with—the envelope system.

My grandmother, Opal, operated on this system. Every payday, she would sit at the well-worn dining table and bring out her box of envelopes. She then would break out her cashed paycheck into envelopes labeled with different categories: rent, utilities, groceries, savings, etc. Every dollar was given a purpose because money without purpose tends to wander away. When it came to paying a bill, she'd go to the envelope and pull out the money to pay the bills. The result is that she had the money to pay for her overhead and some of the extras.

Imagine putting that to work in your business. The profit plan does that as simply as possible. To explain it, it has three components:

Expenses

These are the costs of running the business, which we forecast for the Cost of Goods Sold & Labor (COGS). These are direct costs that happen only when there is work. We also forecast overhead expenses, such as utilities, payroll, marketing, rent, etc. We subtract this from the cash deposits of the month, and what is left over—essentially, your net income or profit—is put to work.

Non-Negotiables

The next component is what must be done. This often includes taxes, reserves, owners' compensation, debt servicing, and a 401(k) or other type of long-term investment. The money left over will fund our desires.

The Desires

This component is the "heart" of the plan. This money is given the intention for things we desire to happen. Typically, this component funds business culture, employee bonuses, charitable contributions, conferences, and continuing education. It can also be where you fund buying a building or setting aside money to reinvest in your business.

Managing profit in this way teaches the brain to assume there will be profits. We are setting intentions and setting the scene. Then, the money is divided, and each element is given a share so that we can fund this *and* that. We minimize surprises and fund the extras.

The results are nothing short of amazing. Not worrying about how you will pay taxes or pay down debt is a huge relief. Imagine the joy of funding the fun as well. Many of our clients use this tool to set aside money to fund benefits or pay raises. A recent client set aside money to travel abroad for ten days for an industry conference. Another client used it to take off an entire month for her honeymoon. The profit plan fulfills the musts, the needs, and the wants while building financial stability.

As we've learned, profit and cash are different. It's great to have intention, but when you start to build reserves with the profit plan, how do you know there will be cash in the bank?

Implementing a Predictive Cash Flow

That's where a *predictive* cash flow comes in and acts like the road map for your business. It is where your budget, fixed costs, incoming client payments, and expected sales pipeline come together.

For years, I kept a 13-week Cash Flow Excel spreadsheet. While inexpensive, it was difficult to maintain because it constantly required me to check if expenses had cleared. Over time, the file kept getting corrupted, and eventually, I just gave up because it was too much work.

In recent years, I have typically recommended an online software solution that automates the process of reconciling bank accounts. I like one that allows scenarios to be added to see the future consequences of a money move today and can show a daily cash flow predictor for a number of years.

The beauty of a system like this is that it allows us to see the anticipated balance of our business accounts **every single day of the year**. Imagine you need to purchase a new computer unexpectedly. It's not within your budget, and your main worry is, is now the time to buy? What may happen in the future if you make this purchase today?

If your only tool is manual, then you open your bank account, reconcile it for outstanding transactions, and try to account for future money coming in, maybe you can be accurate for a few weeks. What happens in a month, or if something doesn't go to plan?

With the predictive online tool, you simply add the expense and scan the calendar view to see its impact. You can see what will happen tomorrow, next month and even next year. The tool allows you to make strategic decisions with greater confidence.

Simply put, start this plan to become an owl as soon as possible—it will be one of the best gifts you can give yourself.

Becoming a better money manager is simple, especially when you have the tools and a system to manage your money and make strategic decisions to build financial stability. Even with these tools in place, if you've struggled with cash flow, these systems will help you understand the true impact of those problems. While humbling, awareness informs you how to fix the issues, which often means we can turn our eyes to profitability.

Chapter 4

BUSINESS MODEL ROADMAP
Creating Your Profitable Path

"Your business model should be
a reflection of your deepest values, your mission,
and your vision for the future."
—Unknown

Many entrepreneurs struggle with choosing the right business model that aligns with their goals and values or creating a pricing strategy that accurately reflects the value they offer. This often leads to inconsistent revenue, underpricing, and missed opportunities.

Your business model should serve as a strategic framework that outlines what products or services the business will sell, how it will market them, who its customers are, and how it expects to generate profit. By aligning your business model with your North Star, you ensure that every decision supports your overarching vision and goals, paving the way for sustainable success.

This chapter will empower you to structure your business with clarity and precision, setting yourself up for sustained profitability. You'll learn to confidently pursue opportunities that align with your goals, knowing exactly when to say yes and when to decline. With a well-chosen model and a pricing strategy that reflects your value, you'll build a business that delivers the lifestyle and impact you envision while bringing unparalleled value to your customers.

Launching My Entrepreneurial Journey:
How I Started My Business

I started my first business in 2007. I was an accidental entrepreneur. Right before opening my first business, I worked for a small business. On May 2, my employer told me I wouldn't have a job as of Friday. She assured me that I did a great job. She simply didn't have the money to keep paying me. I decided I was done and wanted control of my destiny. I called a business lawyer to form a business, wrote a business plan over the weekend, and opened my business on May 7, 2007.

I had a lot to learn. Entrepreneurship is the best example of on-the-job training. Every day is a day you haven't experienced before, forcing you into a mode of constant learning.

What I didn't consider was the business model I was choosing. I had a business plan but did not know my business model. It's like I knew what house I wanted to build but did not have a good foundation to build it on. It's obviously more complicated than that, but you get the idea.

When I started my first business, I looked at my competition and priced my services just slightly lower than theirs. I figured with the lower pricing, I could get my business off and running.

I quickly learned I had set up my business as a low-cost leader and wasn't making any money. I needed a better business model.

What is a Business Model?

When you hear "business model," think of it as how your business will *create*, *deliver*, and *capture* value. You create and deliver value to your clients in the solutions and products you give to others. Then, you "capture value" by receiving payment.

Alexander Osterwalder and Yves Pigneur, the co-founders of Strategyzer, are the leaders of the framework for a good business model. They are recognized for creating the "Business Model Canvas," a powerful tool for analyzing and mapping out the key components of a business model. While variations and evolutions exist, every discussion on business models returns to this pivotal work. This work has made it into the lexicon of business development and will serve as the basis for our conversation moving forward.

Bringing the Business Model Concept
to Your Business

When you first started your business, you might not have realized how valuable it could be to create a business model because, in essence, you were your business model. You could start your business with your ideas, energy, and direct interactions. However, after a few years, redefining what you do and how you do it becomes crucial.

As your business grows and evolves, so do the complexities. A clear, strategic business model becomes invaluable. It brings clarity and structure, helping you articulate and comprehensively map your business processes and strategies. This clarity is not just for you but for your entire team, ensuring everyone is on the same page.

When you create a strategic business model, you enhance clarity so that your team can understand and visualize the key components of your business. It also helps create strategic alignment to ensure that all parts of your business work toward the same goals. Furthermore, it helps you share your vision and strategy, fostering better collaboration.

When you have a defined business model, you can easily identify areas where improvement is needed and operations can be streamlined. Together, this creates a solid foundation that supports growth and adapts to changes.

Harness the Power of Profitability
with the Business Model

The business model is divided into three segments and has nine building blocks. Once we understand the elements, we will walk through defining your business model together.

Segment 1: Desirability or Creating Value

This segment concerns the marketability of your product or service and is divided into four blocks. It seeks to answer the question: What is the market for our product or service?

Value Proposition: What is the compelling value you provide?

Customer Relationships: How do you interact?

Channels: How will you reach or find your customers?

Customer Segments: Who do you help?

Segment 2: Feasibility or Delivering Value

Because this segment is about delivering value, it typically covers logistics and operations and is broken into three blocks. It seeks to answer the question: Do we have the resources to make this doable?

Key Partners: Who will help you?

Key Activities: How will you do it?

Key Resources: What do you need to make it happen?

Segment 3: Viability or Receiving Value

This segment is about receiving value through revenue generation and profitability within two blocks. It seeks to answer the question: How will this be profitable?

Cost Structure: What will it cost to make things happen?

Revenue Streams: How will you make money?

Although it was mentioned last in the segment order, the first thing we tackle is defining how you plan to make money.

This may seem like we are skipping steps, but defining which revenue model you will use will influence the rest of the work in your business model and will save you from needing to rework the business model later.

How will you make money?

Understanding your revenue path is fundamental, as the major segments of your business model will be designed to support this.

When talking about revenue models, we're referring to how your business will capture value—in terms of money—from your clients.

Let's explore four popular revenue models that are used when launching your business or introducing new offerings within your existing setup. These revenue models will help you define your business model's "receive" segment.

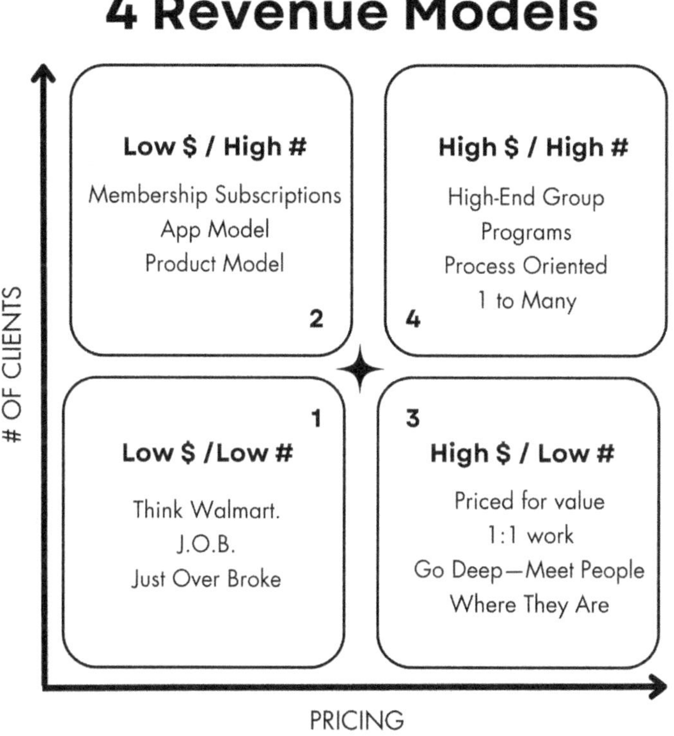

This chart outlines four revenue models based on two key factors: the revenue generated per customer (Low $ vs. High $) and the number of customers (Low # vs. High #).

If a new business owner says, "I'm going to be the cheapest thing out there so that everyone wants to buy from me," they are looking at Revenue Model #1. We've also heard, "I'm going to launch a group program and make millions of dollars." This business owner is likely looking at Revenue Model #4. Typically, businesses go to these two extremes but don't understand that there can be other profitable ways to run a business. For this reason, it's important for us to cover these models to give you the opportunity to make the best decisions for your business.

Revenue Model 1 - Low Price/Low Volume

As I said previously, many businesses initially adopt this revenue model, setting low prices to draw in a large number of customers. As you might recall, that's what I did in my first business. I looked at my competitors and charged less.

The strategy hinges on the hope that a high sales volume will translate into overall profitability.

However, one oversight in this approach is that high sales volume doesn't always compensate for low profit margins. This dilemma is summed up well with the words, "You can't make up in volume what you lose in margin." In other words, even if you sell a lot, the small profit on each item might not add up to enough to keep the business viable.

This revenue model often doesn't generate substantial income for new businesses and can essentially create what's known as a J.O.B. (Just Over Broke) situation—earning barely enough to avoid being broke. It's particularly unsustainable for service-based businesses.

If a business cannot scale, is overwhelmed by customer demand, or is financially strained from hiring necessary support, it's likely trapped in this unprofitable revenue model. It can feel like slogging through sticky clay, where each step forward gets harder.

From my experience across industries, businesses that stick with this low-price, high-volume approach rarely achieve long-term success. It often leads to burnout and is not advisable for anyone aiming to build a profitable, lasting business.

Revenue Model 2 - Low Price/High Volume

This revenue model is about keeping costs low and selling as much as possible. It's perfect for businesses like subscription services, educational platforms, or even book sales. The goal is to get many repeat purchases, which help stabilize your cash flow.

Building a large customer base takes time and dedication. It's about the long game—making small, steady gains until you reach a critical mass of customers. This approach is popular across various industries.

For example, it is often seen in tech or media that lend themselves naturally to a low-price, high-volume revenue model. It also includes health and wellness programs because they provide a steady income stream and build customer loyalty. The challenge is that it can take years to build to a critical mass, and most businesses do not have the cash to stay in the game long enough.

Managing this revenue model effectively means setting up simple, efficient systems to handle everything from client management to project workflows. These systems should be easy to replicate and scale up as your customer base grows.

I recently worked with a client who was launching a new educational platform. Together, we set clear financial targets and calculated how many subscribers she needed to reach her revenue goal of $1,000,000. This initial planning helped us understand when she could expect a return on her investment. We also planned out her staffing needs based on expected subscriber numbers, setting clear milestones for scaling efficiently. All this groundwork was laid before she signed on her first client, ensuring she was well-prepared for growth.

When another client heard about this concept, her eyes lit up! "That's it," she said, "That is what I want to build for my community. That's why I am doing what I am doing. Oh my gosh, this feels so good!" Why did it feel good? Because this owner was called to serve the masses and wants to do it in a way that keeps her services accessible.

Anyone considering this revenue model should think about how you'll deliver your services. Can you automate it, or will it be more hands-on? What kind of systems will you need to support a large number of clients? Before diving in with heavy investments, testing your ideas and understanding your market is essential to avoid the common pitfall of building something perfect for a market that doesn't exist.

Keep it simple at the start. Sell your idea first, then fine-tune your business based on feedback. (This stops Money Trap #1 from occurring.) This revenue model is about adapting quickly and finding what works best for your customers.

Revenue Model 3 - High Price/Low Volume

This revenue model is one of my favorite models when you need to generate significant cash quickly.

If your business helps people or provides something they love, it makes sense to price your services or products to reflect that value. It's not about charging high prices just because you can. If what you offer truly makes a big difference for your customers, then your prices should match that impact. Think about it like this: if you're giving customers a five-star experience, your pricing should reflect that.

The key to success in this revenue model lies in effectively communicating your exceptional value. If you're not attracting the right clients or customers, it is important to reevaluate how you describe your offerings. Adjusting your messaging to be clear and engaging will attract the right audience and make your strategies work more effectively. We will cover this in more detail in Chapter 5.

Some initial improvements may be needed when introducing new products or services. This early phase of this model allows you to refine your offerings based on customer feedback. Each piece of feedback is helpful—it guides you to adjust your products or services and better align with customer preferences. Continuously improving your offerings allows you to set your prices more accurately, attract higher-quality clients, and gradually increase your business's overall value and revenue.

This revenue model largely involves custom work, such as making products tailored to specific customer needs, delivering personalized products, or providing one-on-one services. You could also train a sales team, develop custom software for clients, or even deliver a quick speech on a specific topic.

The key here is to focus on the value you deliver, not just the hours you work. You're offering changes or improvements that make a difference for your clients.

As a word of caution, I would like to remind you that if you don't deliver as promised, your reputation could take a hit, and it might be hard to convince the next client to pay your rates. Since your fees are typically set in advance, you need to be clear about what those fees include and exactly what your clients are getting for their money. Having this laid out helps you keep the project on track and avoid scope creep and profit leaks.

While you don't need to report every hour spent to your clients, you should keep track of your time. Spending more time than planned can reduce your profits. It's also helpful to review your pricing regularly. I recommend checking it quarterly during the first year and then annually afterward.

Revenue Model 4 - High Price/High Volume

This revenue model appeals to the high-end market, where you're looking at both premium prices and a large customer base. You see this in industries like higher education, luxury brands such as Tesla, and upscale resorts that thrive on exclusivity and high value. In the service sector, think about premium mastermind programs that charge $25,000 or more while attracting hundreds of participants annually.

Lululemon Athletica is a well-known example of the High Price/ High Volume revenue model in the athletic apparel industry, appealing particularly to women who value fitness, wellness, and style. Known for its high-quality, stylish yoga pants and workout gear, Lululemon targets professional women willing to pay a premium for comfort, performance, and the brand's aspirational lifestyle appeal. The brand successfully maintains a substantial customer base through its commitment to quality, innovative fabric technology, and community-focused marketing strategies, including yoga classes and running clubs. By fostering a community around its brand and consistently delivering products that resonate with the active, health-conscious woman, Lululemon ensures high sales volumes and cultivates a strong, loyal following, solidifying its position as a premium athletic wear market leader.

Launching with a high-end offering can be an exciting strategy, particularly if you have strong financial backing and a well-recognized brand to attract and retain customers seeking top-notch services or products. If you're just starting out, you might consider building a strong base first and gradually working up to this high-end model. Doing so will allow you to attract customers and grow steadily as your business builds momentum.

This revenue model also works well for businesses with a strong foundation in another model looking to grow or diversify their income after finding success in other areas.

To illustrate these concepts further, let's take a closer look at a fictional business: Tony's Tiny Tacos.

Meet Tony's Tiny Tacos

Tony, a charismatic and slightly eccentric taco enthusiast, wakes up one morning with a revelation. He's convinced that the world needs his secret family taco recipe, and not just any tacos—tiny tacos. Bite-sized bursts of flavor that bring joy to even the grumpiest of taste buds.

With a twinkle in his eye and a stomach full of dreams (*and probably a few too many tacos*), Tony dives headfirst into his new venture. Armed with a food truck he lovingly named "Taco 'Bout Tiny," Tony sets out to share his tiny tacos with the world. His business model? Simple: make tiny tacos, sell tiny tacos, repeat.

For the first few months, Tony is the star of the show. He's the chef, the cashier, the marketing genius with quirky taco-themed puns, and the customer service guru who knows his regulars by name. His infectious enthusiasm and delicious tacos quickly gain a loyal following. Tony's Tiny Tacos becomes a local sensation, and Tony can barely keep up with the demand.

But as the lines grow longer and the taco requests more diverse, Tony realizes something: Running a business isn't just about making great tacos (though that's certainly a big part of it). He needs a real, structured plan that will help him manage the madness, scale his operations, and maybe even take a day off occasionally.

Where Tony's Tiny Tacos Started

Tony started his taco venture with a simple model: high-quality, unique tiny tacos sold directly from his food truck, "Taco 'Bout Tiny." His pricing strategy is accessible, making it easy for many to enjoy his tacos regularly. Initially, Tony's business likely fell into the Revenue Model #2, Low $ / High # quadrant.

Revenue Model #1 Start-up Phase: The Low $ / Low

Many businesses start in Revenue Model #1—Low dollar, Low volume as they price themselves low and must make a name for themselves. However, Tony knew where to place his taco truck and was able to pass by this model and go straight into model #2—still low dollar, but high volume.

Revenue Model #2 Expansion: The Low $ / High

As Tony became competent in his sales, he was able to consider strategically expanding within Revenue Model 2 (Low $ / High #) for several reasons. First, this revenue model has already proven effective and profitable for Tony's Tiny Tacos, so replicating a successful formula reduces risk. There is strong market demand for Tony's affordable, delicious tacos, and expanding to new locations allows Tony to capture more of this demand. Additionally, Tony's brand is already well-known and loved, and new food trucks in different locations can leverage existing brand loyalty and awareness.

Moreover, Tony can use his established systems and processes, making it easier to manage additional food trucks without significant changes. This approach can also lead to economies of scale, with cost savings through bulk purchasing and streamlined operations, further increasing profitability. By adding more food trucks, Tony can reach new customers, increase revenue, and continue to grow his business while maintaining the successful elements that have made Tony's Tiny Tacos a local favorite.

There are two ways he can easily expand within this revenue model: through a subscription option or by adding another food truck. Let's look at each one:

Subscription Option

Tony could introduce a "Taco Club" subscription service, where loyal customers pay a monthly fee for a certain number of tacos or special deals.

This revenue model provides steady, predictable income and strengthens customer loyalty.

Duplication Option: Add a Second Food Truck

Tony continues to sell a high volume of affordable tiny tacos directly from his food truck. However, he adds another food truck in a different location to increase his reach and customer base. This option allows Tony to replicate his successful revenue model, capturing more market share and increasing revenue through higher volume.

Revenue Model #3 Expansion: The High $ / Low

Let's say Tony wanted to expand into Revenue Model #3 (High $ / Low #). He could create different opportunities to bring in high revenue while catering to low amounts of people.

Pay-Per-Use Option

Tony could cater private events or parties, charging based on the number of tacos consumed or the event's size. Provides flexibility and scalability, appealing to customers who want customized catering services.

Revenue Model #4 Expansion: The High $ / High

If Tony instead wanted to reach a lot of people at a high price, he has options in manufacturing, retail, franchising, and licensing.

Manufacturing and Retail Option

Tony could package and sell his unique taco ingredients or ready-to-cook taco kits in gourmet grocery stores. This revenue model allows Tony to reach a premium market that is willing to pay more for high-quality, unique taco products without needing a vast customer base.

Franchising Option

Tony could franchise his food truck business, allowing others to operate their own "Taco 'Bout Tiny" trucks under his brand. This revenue model scales Tony's brand rapidly, generating high revenue from franchise fees and royalties while maintaining high customer volume across multiple locations.

Licensing Option

Tony could license his secret family recipe to other food trucks or restaurants, earning a fee for each location that uses his recipe. This revenue model expands the reach of Tony's Tiny Tacos without the need for direct management of new locations.

Strategic Planning for Tony's Expansion

By understanding his current revenue model and exploring these new options, Tony can strategically plan for expansion. Here's how Tony might approach this:

Identify Core Strengths: Tony's unique taco recipe and charismatic brand are his core strengths. Any expansion should leverage these assets.

Choose the Right Revenue Model: Depending on his goals, Tony might choose a combination of the above revenue models. For instance, he could launch a subscription service while exploring licensing and manufacturing opportunities.

Align Business Segments: As Tony defines the major segments of his revenue model, he'll ensure each segment supports his chosen revenue models, from sourcing ingredients to marketing strategies.

What About Your Business?

Reflect on how you first began to capture value and where you envision your business moving in the future. Each revenue model we've discussed has unique strengths and challenges tailored for different types of market engagements and growth phases. Whether you prefer a subscription revenue model's high scalability or a product-based setup's stability, your choice must align with your long-term business goals and current market position.

The right revenue model can dramatically shorten your path to profitability. It reduces initial risks and lays a solid foundation for scalability. Imagine launching with a revenue model that perfectly aligns with your market's needs—how much quicker could you reach your financial targets?

Consider the power of strategic diversification. Once your initial revenue model is firmly established and generating profit, exploring additional revenue models can protect and enhance your business against market shifts. This isn't about shifting strategies on a whim; it's about thoughtful expansion into new arenas that complement your existing successes, ensuring you capture a wider audience and create multiple revenue streams.

Think of your business as a tree. Your primary revenue model is the trunk, sturdy and supportive. Diversifying adds branches, spreading your reach and influence. This approach not only solidifies your core operations but also provides stability and resilience in the face of market changes.

Your Next Steps

To take practical steps forward, here are two actions you can take:

1. **Assess Your Current Revenue Model:** Revisit your business revenue model and evaluate its strengths and weaknesses. Identify which revenue model you currently use and consider if it best fits your business goals.
2. **Explore New Revenue Models:** Research and brainstorm how other revenue models could enhance your business. For example, could a subscription revenue model offer steady income? Could licensing your product or service expand your reach? Consider how these revenue models could complement your existing operations.

By strategically aligning and expanding your business revenue model, you'll be well-equipped to achieve sustainable success. These steps will help you solidify your core operations while exploring new opportunities for growth and profitability.

As you consider these steps and explore new revenue models, it's essential to understand the client value proposition, which we will discuss in the next chapter. We'll look into developing a compelling client value proposition, showing what sets you apart from the competition and how to communicate that to your target audience. This will not only attract more customers but also ensure that your business continues to thrive and grow.

Chapter 5

WINNING CUSTOMERS
Crafting Value Propositions
That Drive Conversions

"The aim of marketing is to know and
understand the customer so well the product
or service fits them and sells itself."
—Peter Drucker

Have you ever stood in line for concert tickets, sporting events, or even the latest technology release of your favorite device? Brands with cult-like followings are often brands with incredible client value propositions.

Brands like Apple, Tesla, Taylor Swift, Coca-Cola, and Whataburger have built such brand loyalty that their clients are nothing short of raving fans.

We are talking about your business's value proposition and how the strength of your value position directly supports its profitability.

What is a Client Value Proposition?

A Client Value Proposition (CVP) is the promise of value the business intends to deliver to its clients. It is a crucial part of our business foundation strategy for profitable growth. This statement helps your customers choose your business over the competition and pay your price in exchange for that value.

Think of the CVP as the core reason customers should choose you. It's not just about the products or services you offer—those are the means to deliver something more significant. The Client Value Proposition (CVP) includes:

Value is what your customers get from choosing your product or service. It includes both tangible benefits like product features and intangible benefits like how it makes them feel. This value is why your customers come to you in the first place, and it's often what they think about, consciously and unconsciously, when they decide to buy.

Relevance communicates how you solve the problem for your client and the payoff for solving that problem. It tells the before-and-after story for your client—how their life or business is better after finding your solution. Relevance connects the dots for customers and shows them the direct benefits of choosing you.

Differentiation communicates your unique selling proposition to your ideal client and can help them decide to choose your company over the competition. This is your ability to stand out and help your ideal customers understand why they should pick you over anyone else.

An effective CVP is important because it forms the foundations for so many elements of success. A clear value proposition provides clarity of purpose and helps everyone on the team understand what you stand for and offer. This clarity simplifies marketing and expansion strategies, offering further refinement to guide all strategic decisions.

This clarity further improves your position in the market, customer attraction, and retention. Your ideal client understands what you'll do for them and has less objection to buying from you. The CVP effectively sells the client and lowers price sensitivity. The perfect illustration is when a potential client says, "I know it is more expensive, but it is worth it."

In essence, the client value proposition is a statement about your products or services that reflects how well the business understands your clients' desires and how well you fulfill them. It is what makes you the best choice for the job.

Most businesses start without this work defined. For a while, it works because, for the first few years, you can activate your personal network to obtain your initial clients. Basically, YOU are your value proposition. These people already know, like, and trust you. The initial clients are willing to take a risk because of that trust.

It continues to work when those original clients refer to others because the referral clients trust the friend that referred you and likely spoke of their personal experience with greater clarity than you can achieve on your own.

As you look to master more profitable growth and need to extend past your network to develop clients who may not be familiar with your work, this foundational element becomes even more important.

Signs That You Need To Improve Your CVP

Before we dive into the steps for defining your Client Value Proposition (CVP), let's examine the external factors that might signal the need to create or refine your CVP.

Market Confusion: If customers or potential customers struggle to understand what your business does or how it differs from competitors, your CVP isn't clear enough. This confusion can hinder sales, damage brand perception, and even make customers more price-sensitive.

Competitive Pressure: When new competitors enter the market or existing ones enhance their offerings, a strong CVP becomes crucial. If your offerings get lost in the crowd, it's time to revisit and strengthen your value proposition.

Customer Retention Issues: If you're losing customers despite maintaining quality products or services, a weak CVP could be to blame. Additionally, this could indicate that your customer experience isn't effectively reinforcing the value you promise.

Evolving Target Audience: As your ideal customer profile evolves, your CVP needs to keep pace. Refining your value proposition ensures it resonates with your target audience's changing needs and preferences.

Business Growth or Expansion: A strong CVP is essential for sustainable growth. It's the heartbeat of your company, drawing in customers and fostering loyalty. When expanding your services or entering new markets, ensure your CVP remains the guiding force behind your strategies.

In summary, your CVP is the foundation upon which your business's success is built. It should clearly articulate the unique value you offer, resonate with your ideal customers, and differentiate you from the competition. As you plan for growth, ensure all your efforts align with your core values and mission, building upon the strong foundation you've established.

In simpler terms, it's like making sure that as your business grows, it still feels like the same business that people originally loved, with more to offer.

Think of your value proposition as your compass, guiding each decision and ensuring that every new adventure is still distinctly "you," allowing your business to grow bigger and better. In this way, the CVP adds to your North Star to guide who you serve and how your business impacts the world.

A strong brand connection is a key component of a compelling CVP. Brands that excel in creating this connection often share several characteristics: a strong identity, a sense of community, exceptional customer experience, exclusivity, and an emotional bond with their customers. Let's explore how one brand, facing a significant marketing challenge, was able to refine its CVP to take a new product from unknown to household staple.

The Febreze Marketing Problem

In my advertising agency days, I had the privilege of working with many big brand managers at consumer goods companies. These brand managers had a unique relationship with their brands. They viewed themselves as guardians and stewards of their brands, almost as if the brands were their children.

The managers consistently spoke of the buyer's emotional connection with the brand—this connection was always in the front of their minds. If you will, this was the heart and soul of the brand. On the opposite side of the spectrum was the head. The head was the data machine that supported the brand. Data is the currency that keeps a brand alive. After all, the job of a brand is to create value for the consumer and the company in terms of revenue and profits.

When a new brand comes into the fold, it often has data backing the decision, but it has a limited opportunity to pick up traction in the market. Febreze is one of those products. It was introduced in test markets in 1996 but didn't hit the mainstream market until 1998. That's because the brand almost didn't reach the mainstream market.

The product solves the problem of odor eradication. In science, Febreze encapsulates the odor, therefore reducing the odor. As a mother of two boys and two fur babies, I don't necessarily care about the science—I care if it works. If it can remove the smell of stinky teenager boys, I'm happy.

Let's look at the problem. It's pervasive and constant, and if you can establish a brand relationship, you'll establish a lifetime of purchase renewals.

The product is unique and has little to no competition on the market, so there was a market waiting to be claimed. The product delivered on its brand promise. Yet, the product wasn't catching on. The marketing team struggled to find the emotional connection.

The marketing team was seasoned and smart. Having worked with Procter & Gamble employees, I know they are all highly intelligent. Why were they struggling to find that emotional connection? Doesn't everyone want a nice-smelling home?

The brand was struggling to gain momentum and was running out of time. To find an answer, the team went directly to the consumer and began asking questions.

Did the product work? "Oh, yes. Very well."

Did you use it a second time? "No."

Why? "I forgot that I had it."

Isn't that intriguing? It shows the lack of a relationship between the product and the user. Have you ever had a client tell you they forgot that your business took care of the service they hired another company for?

The team decided to try one last time. In this last market test, the marketing team asked the consumer for permission to install cameras in certain areas of their homes. The test asked the consumer to use the product for two weeks. The team then scoured the footage, searching for the answer, and the simplest action began to repeat in the homes, time and time again. After cleaning or tidying up a room, the consumer would spray Febreze in it. Once they put down the product, they inhaled deeply and viewed the room with satisfaction. This simple action was repeated over and over again. They found the missing piece.

The next time you see a commercial for the Febreze brand, watch for the inhale and then a smile of satisfaction. It is in every advertisement.

In this case, the emotional connection is the sense of satisfaction of a job well done. In that brief moment, the consumer is a hero over smell.

The Febreze case study reminds us that the most compelling aspects of a CVP might not always be obvious. It's easy to focus on the functional benefits of a product or service, but the emotional connection often lies in the simplest, most fundamental aspects of the customer experience. Let's unpack the steps to define your CVP, keeping in mind that the most powerful value propositions often go beyond the obvious.

The Steps To Defining Your
Client Value Proposition (CVP)

Developing a strong Client Value Proposition (CVP) is key to building a profitable business. It's the foundation for attracting ideal clients and fostering lasting customer relationships. But finding the emotional connection that truly resonates can be challenging. If you're unsure where to start, let's break down the process into manageable steps.

Step 1. Define the Value You Provide

There are three main items to define to have clients easily say yes to what you are selling. You need to define:

1. The Reasons to Buy
2. The Client's Journey
3. How You Deliver the Value

Defining Your Clients' Reasons to Buy

To understand why people buy, let's look at a modern example of Maslow's Hierarchy of Needs. Abraham Maslow was an American psychologist who developed Maslow's Hierarchy of Needs in the early 20th century. According to Maslow's theory, human motivations and needs must be satisfied sequentially, beginning with the basic needs and culminating with transcendence. As we have refined this technique for our clients, the similarity between reasons to buy and Maslow's Hierarchy of Needs highlighted a parallel that we can use to our advantage.

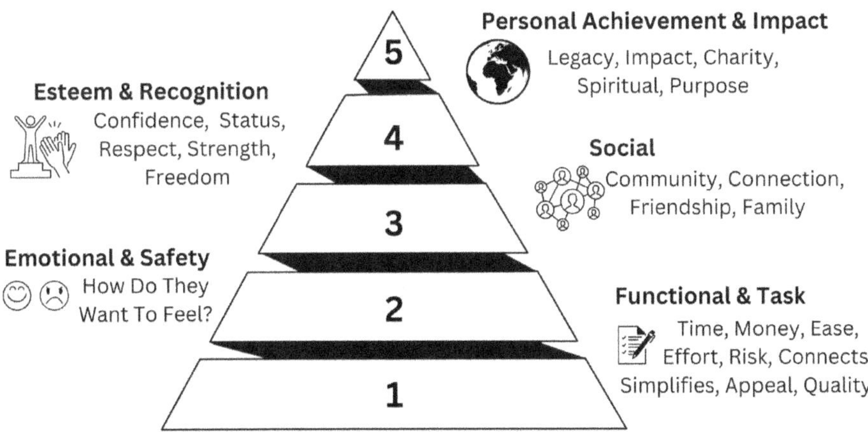

Understanding the Hierarchy of Needs in terms of a house may be helpful. Our house has functional and task, emotional, social, esteem and recognition, and personal achievement and impact needs.

Biological needs are basic *Functional and Task* needs, such as food, water, and shelter. They are the must-haves for survival. *Emotional and*

Safety needs include physical, mental, and financial security, health, and stability. It's like making sure that your house has locks and is in a good, safe neighborhood. It also includes how we as individuals feel. These first two needs do not include aesthetics. Those will come later.

Now that we have a home and are safe, let's share it. The third level involves *Social* needs and includes friends, family, romantic relationships, a sense of belonging, and feeling loved within a community. Once we have our house filled with family and friends, it's warm and welcoming.

The next level of needs, and still in the foundational elements of our house, is *Esteem and Recognition* needs. Once you feel loved and secure, you might focus on feeling good about yourself and gaining the respect of others. Esteem is often equated to the pursuit of success, confidence, and pride in one's accomplishments. Maybe this is where "Yard of the Month" becomes important.

Then there's the final level of *Personal Achievement and Impact*. Perhaps achieving the recognition of others for your home has been transformational and you know you want to help others achieve the same thing. Perhaps you now believe that it is a core human right to have a home that you create a non-profit to facilitate affordable housing. This final level is more about creating a legacy.

Think of Maslow's Hierarchy of Needs as a roadmap to understand why people buy. From basic needs like food and shelter to personal growth and fulfillment, this framework helps us see what motivates our clients to choose one product or service over another.

The strongest value propositions tap into these fundamental human desires, guiding our marketing and sales strategies to address what matters most to our customers directly. By aligning our offers with the needs in Maslow's hierarchy, we can build compelling messages that resonate deeply and increase the likelihood of people buying from us.

You can use this concept to refine your value proposition and connect more effectively with your clients. We recommend breaking down the reasons to buy into three categories: logical, emotional, and aspirational. As you work through this process, you'll brainstorm and end up with nine potential reasons to buy.

The Functional and Logical Reasons to Buy

When selling your product or service, there are straightforward, logical reasons why a client might decide to buy from you. These are what we call the functional reasons. These are the practical, nuts-and-bolts reasons someone would choose your product or service and show the *logical* reasons someone would buy from you.

For your business, determine three functional/logical reasons someone would want to buy from you. Consider the specifics: If it's a product, how does it outperform competitors in durability, efficiency, or cost savings? If it's a service, how does it streamline operations, save time, or improve reliability for your clients?

Include quality because while this can still be subjective, it is an expectation that every client has when they engage with your business. As a general rule, avoid adding "experience." Experience can come back into the value proposition. Experience, such as the statement, "More than 35 years experience as…" is more about you and less about your client. Focus on the outcome or benefit that your clients would receive as a result of that experience. Does your experience create value by being error-free? Does it save the client time and money because you are efficient?

These foundational benefits are essential as they form the initial reason a client would consider your offering. Then, layer on additional specific benefits that set you apart from the competition. Focusing on these practical reasons creates a logical argument that makes it easy for customers to see why your offering is the right choice. This approach appeals to their rational side and explains why they can't afford to pass up your product or service.

The Emotional and Social Reasons to Buy

There are emotional and social reasons a client will choose to buy from you. They will lean on these heartfelt and communal motivations to feel good about their decision. These feelings and social benefits make someone not just choose but love your product or service.

For your business, come up with three emotional reasons someone would buy from you. Consider factors like prestige, community belonging, or emotional satisfaction. Another one could be the sense of pride one feels from owning your product, as that often resonates deeply. You might highlight an aspect of your offering that enhances personal joy or social status. It's like opting for a luxury car not just for the ride but for the status it confers—these are the compelling and resonant reasons to prefer one option over another.

The Esteem, Recognition, Achievement, and Impact Reasons to Buy

Whereas up to now, you may have found it easy to determine your reasons to buy, this last section may be more challenging. Again, we want to brainstorm three reasons to buy that are applicable to the upper levels of the Hierarchy of Needs. Consider the following questions to help uncover why your client buys:

- How does owning or using your product/service make your customers feel more accomplished?
- What are the shareable aspects of your product/service that customers would likely boast about on social media or in person?
- How does your product/service enable customers to help others achieve their goals?

Once you have defined three reasons in each section, you now have a list of nine potential reasons to buy. Do you need that many? Probably not. In fact, if you can reduce them to a core group of four, it will be easier to share them with others.

You can test your theory by listing your top ten clients. Using your list of reasons to buy, consider why each client purchased from you. Write down the reasons for each client to buy. Once you have completed your list, which ones stand out? What are the reasons they all share, and where do they differ? Once we have this understanding, we can move on to step two of defining your relevant value propositions—defining the client journey.

Step 2. Identify the Client's Journey

We begin to map out the client's journey by looking at our ideal client. It is possible that your ideal client is not just one type of persona but has multiple personas. In the context of marketing, personas are fictional representations of your ideal customers. They are detailed profiles that reflect variations in preferences, behaviors, and needs within a target audience. Creating personas helps businesses tailor their marketing efforts to specific customer segments, allowing for more personalized and effective communication. For instance, if you run a fitness coaching business, your ideal client could be represented by multiple personas: a busy professional looking for quick, effective workouts, a new parent trying to get back into shape, or a retired individual focusing on health and mobility.

If this is the case, choose the most dominant persona and go through the process. Then, repeat it for any other personas. The exercise you just completed, where you listed your top ten past clients, will often help in this exercise.

Once each persona is clearly defined, outline their journey. Think of this journey as a before-and-after story. For the busy professional, the "before" might involve struggling to fit exercise into a hectic schedule and feeling constantly stressed and out of shape. The "after" shows how, with your tailored short workout programs, they can manage fitness effectively, leading to improved health and more personal time.

As you craft these narratives, the goal is to vividly paint the picture of your ideal client's life before discovering your solution. This not only helps create a compelling marketing message but also ensures that the solutions we provide resonate deeply with each persona's specific challenges and desires. Through these detailed, persona-specific journeys, we can more effectively communicate how your services transform their lives, making the value of your solution immediately apparent.

To start defining this journey, we need to understand our clients' core challenges. Let's begin by defining the problem they are facing, the one they seek to solve.

Define the Problem

Understanding your ideal client's problem is the cornerstone of a strong CVP. We need to dig deep, exploring not just the surface-level issue but the underlying causes and how they impact your client's life.

Start by asking:

- What problem brings clients to your door? This is the most immediate, visible issue they're trying to solve.
- Why is this a problem? Explore the consequences and negative impacts of this problem. What does it cost them emotionally, financially, or otherwise?
- What's the root cause? Keep asking "why" to uncover deeper layers. Often, the initial problem is a symptom of a more fundamental challenge.

As an example, suppose you're a career coach. A client might come to you wanting to land a better job (the visible problem). But why is this a problem? Perhaps they feel stuck and undervalued in their current role (the consequences). Digging deeper, you might discover they lack confidence in their skills or struggle to articulate their value (the root cause).

By thoroughly exploring the problem, its root causes, and its manifestations, you gain a deep understanding of your client's needs and motivations. This understanding allows you to tailor your CVP to resonate with their specific challenges and desires, making your solution more compelling and effective.

Define the Pain

To truly understand your client's needs and create a compelling message, it's crucial to explore the pain caused by their problem. This isn't about exploiting their struggles; it's about fostering awareness and highlighting the value of your solution. Consider these key questions:

- What does the pain feel like? Describe the emotional and practical impact of the problem. Is it frustration, anxiety, wasted time, or financial loss?
- What is the intensity of the pain? Is it a mild annoyance or a major obstacle? How frequently does it occur, and how long does it last?

- What are the consequences of not addressing the pain? What will your client miss out on or suffer if the problem persists? Will it worsen over time?

Remember, clients might be so accustomed to their pain that they've become numb to it. This is where your expertise comes in. By vividly illustrating the pain and its consequences, you can rekindle their awareness and motivation to seek a solution.

For example, the Febreze marketing team discovered that many pet owners had become "nose blind" to lingering odors in their homes. By highlighting this common issue and demonstrating the transformative power of Febreze, they successfully awakened a need and drove product adoption.

Paint the Picture of Transformation: The Promise and Payoff

Now that we've explored the problem and the pain, it's time to shift the focus to the positive. This is where you showcase the transformative power of your solution. Imagine your ideal client after they've experienced your product or service.

How do they feel? Describe the emotional shift. Are they relieved, confident, empowered?

What positive outcomes have they achieved? Highlight the tangible benefits and results they've gained.

What does their life look like now? Paint a vivid picture of their transformed reality.

This is where your earlier work on "Reasons to Buy" becomes invaluable. Connect the dots between your solution and the positive outcomes your clients experience. Show them how your product or service directly contributes to their desired transformation.

Remember, this is your opportunity to inspire and motivate. By vividly describing the positive outcomes and painting a compelling picture of the "after" state, you create a powerful emotional connection. You show potential clients that their desired transformation is not only possible but within reach with your help.

Step 3. How Will You Deliver Value?

Now that you have defined the value you provide and mapped out the client journey, it's time to focus on how you will deliver this value effectively and consistently. A well-defined plan builds trust and loyalty, ensuring a seamless and satisfying client experience.

Define the Plan

Clearly outline the core aspects of your offering and how they address your client's problems and pain points. Aim to convey your expertise and ability to guide them successfully. While clients want to know what's included, avoid overwhelming them with excessive detail. Instead, focus on these key elements:

Core Offering: Briefly describe the main services or products included in your solution.

Key Features: Highlight the most important features or benefits that directly address the client's needs.

Process Overview: Provide a high-level overview of your process, demonstrating a clear and logical approach.

Timeline or Milestones: If applicable, outline a general timeline or key milestones to set expectations.

Remember, the plan is about showing you have a structured approach, not about listing every detail. For example, instead of listing all 50 points of a technical inspection, simply stating "50-Point Inspection by Licensed Technicians" conveys the thoroughness and expertise clients can expect.

Focus on the Outcome, Not the Work

Avoid the common pitfall of overemphasizing the work involved. Clients don't want more work; they want results. Frame your plan in terms of the outcomes and benefits they'll experience, keeping the focus on the "What's In It For Me?" factor.

Here are some key considerations:

Clarity: Use clear and concise language, avoiding jargon or overly technical terms.

Client-Centric: Focus on the benefits and outcomes for the client, not just the tasks you'll perform.

Conciseness: Provide enough detail to build trust and understanding, but avoid overwhelming with unnecessary information.

Alignment: Ensure your plan directly supports the problem, pain, and promise you've defined.

By following these guidelines, you can create a plan that effectively communicates the value you deliver and sets clear expectations for your clients. This builds confidence in your ability to guide them through their transformation journey.

Step 4. Drafting the Yes Formula

Now that you understand your client's problems and pain points, have presented a solution, and outlined a plan, it's time to weave these elements together into a persuasive narrative. This narrative, known as the "Yes Formula," will be the core of your messaging, guiding how you communicate your unique value to potential clients.

The Yes Formula is simple:

*(**Problem x Pain x Promise) + Plan > Change or Investment**

This formula emphasizes that the problem, pain, and promise are the most impactful parts of your message. They represent the "before" and "after" states for your client, creating a compelling case for change. The plan, while important, plays a supporting role, outlining how you'll deliver the promised transformation.

To effectively communicate your Yes Formula, consider using the Accordion Strategy. This strategy recognizes that your messaging needs to be flexible. Sometimes, a concise, impactful message is needed (like an elevator pitch). Other times, a more detailed explanation is appropriate (like a sales presentation).

Think of your Yes Formula as an accordion. You can compress it for quick, impactful delivery or expand it for a deeper dive, depending on the situation. This flexibility ensures that your message is always clear, persuasive, and tailored to your audiences.

The Problem, Pain, and Promise

Now that you've learned the formula, put it into action! Once you've used it a few times, you'll wonder how you ever managed without it. Remember, to motivate a client to change or invest, they must see that the solution you offer is far better than their current situation.

At our company, we use this formula ourselves. Our marketing and sales strategies are built around a deep understanding of our ideal clients. To see this in action, check out our *Profitable Growth for Business* newsletter on LinkedIn. You'll find hundreds of articles addressing the problems our clients face. As you read, try to identify the problem, pain, and promise we highlight in each one.

Defining your CVP is crucial because it impacts every aspect of your business. For example, earlier this year, we helped a client revitalize their growth strategy. They were transitioning out of a foundational building phase and needed to re-energize their team. We worked together to develop a strong CVP, emphasizing the importance of engaging every team member—from the receptionist to the owner—in the marketing process.

Let me share a story about a client who truly embraced the power of crafting a strong CVP. This business was ready to reignite growth but recognized the need for a more focused and energized approach. We started by identifying five distinct personas within their ideal client profile. Remember, while your ideal client represents the core characteristics of your target audience, personas delve deeper, reflecting the nuances in their preferences, behaviors, and needs.

We explored the goals of the ideal client and then tailored value propositions for each persona, considering their unique demographics, pain points, and motivations. The results were transformative. The team felt re-energized and gained a much deeper understanding of their clients and how to serve them effectively.

The owner was then able to work individually with each team member, aligning their marketing and sales efforts with the persona that resonated most with their own life stage or interests. This personalized approach fostered a sense of ownership and enthusiasm within the team.

We didn't stop there. We identified specific opportunities that aligned perfectly with each persona's needs and used these insights to develop a compelling speaking presentation for the owner. The impact was immediate and measurable.

The owner shared, "You wouldn't believe how excited the team is about the persona work. They come into my office after a sales call or meeting with a client, energized that they can recognize the problem, ask questions about the pain, and promise to deliver exactly what our ideal client wants from us. By the way, we've closed three accounts in the last two weeks."

This story illustrates how a well-defined CVP can not only clarify your marketing message but also ignite your team's passion and drive tangible results. Imagine your own team, armed with a deep understanding of your ideal clients and empowered to deliver a tailored, impactful message. The possibilities for growth and success are truly limitless.

How Tony's Tiny Tacos Expanded with a New Client Value Proposition

To understand how a strong client value proposition (CVP) can adapt to different business models and fuel growth, let's revisit Tony's Tiny Tacos. Tony's food truck has been a local sensation, thanks to his unique bite-sized tacos and charismatic presence. Now, Tony aims to expand into the retail market. By exploring how Tony can tailor his CVP to this new venture, we'll demonstrate the versatility and impact of a well-crafted value proposition.

Tony's Client Value Propositions

1. Tony's Current Clients (Food Truck)

Problem: Customers crave a quick, delicious, and unique meal that stands out from typical fast-food options. They desire convenient and flavorful food but struggle to find high-quality, affordable street food.

Pain: Settling for bland, generic fast food leaves customers unsatisfied and disappointed. The lack of unique dining experiences that fit into busy schedules means missing out on enjoying a special meal during a quick lunch break or casual outing.

Promise: Tony's Tiny Tacos offers a delightful and convenient dining experience with signature bite-sized tacos made from a secret family recipe. Unique flavors and friendly service ensure a memorable visit, providing a quick, satisfying meal that fits perfectly into busy lives.

Plan: "Taco 'Bout Tiny," Tony's food truck, is strategically located in high-traffic areas for easy access. High-quality ingredients and a streamlined cooking process ensure fast service without compromising taste. Customers can enjoy their tacos on the go or in the vibrant atmosphere of the food truck, knowing they are getting a unique, flavorful meal.

Value: Tony's Tiny Tacos offers a unique culinary experience with delicious, bite-sized tacos made from a secret family recipe, providing a convenient and flavorful meal that stands out.

Relevance: Tony's Tiny Tacos solves the problem of finding a quick, satisfying, and unique meal for busy professionals, families, and food enthusiasts. Customers experience the joy of delicious food that fits perfectly into their busy lives.

Differentiation: Tony's Tiny Tacos is known for its distinctive tiny tacos, friendly service, and vibrant food truck atmosphere.

The combination of unique flavors, quality ingredients, and Tony's charismatic presence makes it the preferred choice.

Client Value Proposition Statement: Tony's Tiny Tacos offers a delightful and convenient dining experience with signature bite-sized tacos made from a secret family recipe. Unique flavors and friendly service make each visit memorable, providing a quick and satisfying meal for busy individuals and families. Choose Tony's for a food truck experience that stands out.

2. Tony's Manufacturing and Retail Expansion

Problem: Home cooks and taco enthusiasts often struggle to recreate the unique flavors and quality of restaurant-style tacos at home. They desire the convenience of a gourmet taco experience without the hassle of sourcing specialty ingredients or spending excessive time on preparation.

Pain: The disappointment of homemade tacos that don't live up to expectations can be frustrating. Sourcing ingredients, following complex recipes, and the time spent cooking can make the experience more of a chore than a pleasure. This often leads to a less enjoyable dining experience compared to eating out.

Promise: Tony's Tiny Tacos delivers the beloved food truck experience right to your kitchen with our convenient, ready-to-cook taco kits. Enjoy the same unique, bite-sized tacos made with high-quality ingredients and our secret family recipe. Perfect for busy individuals or those who simply love great tacos, our kits make it easy to create restaurant-quality tacos at home.

Plan: Our ready-to-cook taco kits include pre-portioned, high-quality ingredients and easy-to-follow instructions. Simply assemble and cook according to the directions for a delicious, authentic Tony's Tiny Tacos experience in minutes. Our kits are available in gourmet grocery stores and online for ultimate convenience.

Value: Tony's Tiny Tacos ready-to-cook taco kits bring the unique flavors and quality of our food truck to your home, making it easy to recreate our beloved tiny tacos with minimal effort.

Relevance: Our taco kits are perfect for individuals who love the taste of Tony's Tiny Tacos but want the convenience of enjoying them at home. They offer a hassle-free solution for those who crave restaurant-quality tacos without the time and effort of cooking from scratch.

Differentiation: Our taco kits stand out with their unique tiny taco format, high-quality ingredients, and Tony's secret family recipe. They offer a convenient way to experience the authentic Tony's Tiny Tacos taste without waiting in line at the food truck.

Client Value Proposition Statement: Tony's Tiny Tacos brings the beloved food truck experience to your kitchen with our ready-to-cook taco kits. Enjoy the same unique, bite-sized tacos made from high-quality ingredients and our secret family recipe. Perfect for home cooks and taco enthusiasts, our kits make it easy to create restaurant-quality tacos at home. Experience the taste of Tony's Tiny Tacos anytime, without leaving your house.

Putting Your Value Proposition to Work: Action Steps

Crafting a compelling Client Value Proposition (CVP) is essential for business success. It clearly communicates the unique value you offer, attracting ideal clients and fostering growth. To develop your CVP, follow these steps:

1. **Define the Value You Provide:** Identify the core problem you solve, the pain points it causes, the solution you promise, and your plan to deliver it.
2. **Craft Your CVP Statement:** Combine these elements into a clear, concise statement that resonates with your ideal client.
3. **Test and Refine:** Incorporate your CVP into conversations, gather feedback, and continuously improve it.

4. **Implement Across Your Business:** Integrate your CVP into your company culture, strategies, and customer interactions.

Congratulations on Crafting Your Client Value Proposition!

Congratulations on crafting your compelling CVP! By defining your business's value, relevance, and differentiation, you've laid a strong foundation for success. Aligning your operations and messaging with your customers' needs will undoubtedly yield significant rewards.

How do you know your CVP resonates? If it evokes a physical reaction—like mouth watering at the thought of Tony's Tiny Tacos or a sense of excitement and anticipation—you're on the right track. This shows that your value proposition strikes an emotional chord with your audience.

But a compelling CVP is just the beginning of ensuring a strong foundation for your business. Next, we'll dive into the feasibility of your business model. We'll explore the logistics, activities, and partnerships necessary to turn your vision into reality. Get ready to learn how to ensure you have the resources and support to execute your value proposition effectively and build a thriving business.

Chapter 6

TURNING IDEAS INTO REALITY
Key Steps to Business Feasibility

"An idea can only become a reality once it is
broken down into organized, actionable elements."
—Scott Belsky

Have you ever wondered what it takes to turn a brilliant idea into a thriving business? It requires more than just a great concept; it demands careful planning and execution to ensure your idea is not only viable but also sustainable. While some of you may already be familiar with these foundational concepts, this chapter offers a valuable opportunity to revisit them, refine your understanding, and ensure your business is truly operating at its full potential.

This chapter focuses on the feasibility of your business model. We'll explore the essential components that make your business work, including the resources you need, the activities you'll undertake, and the partnerships that can support your success. This will help you assess whether your business idea has the potential to thrive in the real world. To assess feasibility, we need to consider three key questions:

1. **Capabilities:** What activities are essential to your business's success?
2. **Resources:** What physical, financial, intellectual, or human assets are required?
3. **Partners:** Who can provide support or expertise to fill any gaps?

Let's explore each of these areas in more detail.

Capabilities/Key Activities: The Core Activities of Your Business

Every business has a set of core activities that drive its operations and deliver value to customers. These activities can be broadly categorized into several areas:

Production: Creating or manufacturing your product or service.

Problem-Solving: Developing innovative solutions to customer problems.

Platform/Network: Building and maintaining a platform or network that facilitates interactions between users or customers.

For example, a software company's key activities might include software development, quality testing, and customer support. A consulting firm might focus on client acquisition, project management, and knowledge development.

The Benefits of Identifying Your Key Activities

Effective Resource Allocation: Understanding your key activities allows you to channel your time, money, and manpower into the areas that drive the most value. For example, a law firm could dedicate more resources to hiring experienced attorneys and investing in legal research tools. Administrative tasks like document filing and appointment scheduling could be outsourced, allowing attorneys to focus on billable hours.

Building Competitive Advantage: Recognizing where your business's core strengths lie helps you differentiate yourself in the marketplace. For instance, a marketing firm known for its creative campaigns could allocate resources to hiring talented designers and copywriters. This focus would not only set them apart but also reinforce their brand as an innovative marketing solutions provider.

Improving Operational Efficiency: Focusing on essential activities enables you to streamline operations and reduce waste. By honing in on what truly matters, you can eliminate inefficiencies and improve productivity. For example, a manufacturing company might identify its key activities as procurement, production, and quality control. By streamlining these processes through automation and lean manufacturing principles, they can reduce lead times, minimize defects, and increase output.

Continuous Innovation: This strategic focus helps you continuously improve and innovate, further strengthening your business in an everchanging world. For example, a restaurant could regularly collect customer feedback to refine its menu, ambiance, and service. This commitment to innovation would ensure they stay ahead of dining trends and consistently deliver a satisfying customer experience.

As you work on these tasks, keep in mind that later on, you will want to find ways to scale them. Achieving scalability often requires a willingness to embrace unscalable tasks in the beginning. These hands-on, labor-intensive activities typically are not sustainable as your business grows, but they are crucial for building a strong foundation.

Tony's Tiny Tacos Illustrates Key Activities

Take Tony, for example, who personally handled customer service in the early days of Tony's Tiny Tacos. This direct interaction with customers provided invaluable insights into their needs, which informed the scalable systems he implemented later on. It's also essential to have a clear vision for scalability, even when you're immersed in the nitty-gritty of unscalable tasks.

Envision the systems and processes that will streamline your operations and support growth. This foresight ensures a smooth transition from manual efforts to automated, scalable solutions, allowing you to focus on strategic initiatives.

However, it's important to avoid analysis paralysis when planning your core activities. While understanding the details is important, over-emphasizing them can be counterproductive. Think of it like planning a road trip: you need a clear destination and route, but you don't need to map out every single turn.

By maintaining a high-level perspective, you can stay focused on the core activities that truly drive your business forward, preventing you from getting bogged down by less important details. This approach ensures clarity and direction as you work toward your goals.

Once you have a good grasp of the core activities that drive your business, it's important to consider the resources needed to support these activities. These resources are the building blocks that enable your business to function and deliver value to customers.

Key Resources:
The Assets That Drive Your Business

Your key resources are the assets that enable your business to function and deliver value. These resources can be categorized into four main types:

1. **Physical:** Tangible assets like buildings, equipment, or inventory.
2. **Financial:** Capital, credit lines, or other financial instruments.
3. **Intellectual:** Patents, trademarks, copyrights, or brand reputation.
4. **Human:** The skills, knowledge, and experience of your team.

For instance, a manufacturing company might rely heavily on physical resources like factories and machinery. A technology startup might prioritize intellectual resources like patents and software code. A consulting firm's most valuable resource might be its team of experienced consultants. Understanding your key resources is essential for:

Strategic Planning: It helps you identify which resources are critical to your business model and where you might need to invest or acquire additional assets.

Risk Management: Knowing your resource dependencies allows you to assess potential risks and develop mitigation strategies.

Value Creation: Leveraging your unique resources can help you create a competitive advantage and deliver superior value to customers.

Understanding your key resources is fundamental, but it's equally important to recognize that you don't have to go it alone. Strategic partnerships can provide access to additional resources, expertise, and support, enhancing your business model and accelerating your growth.

Key Partners: Building a Supportive Ecosystem

No business operates in isolation. Strategic partnerships can provide valuable support, expertise, and resources that enhance your business model. Key partners can be categorized into several types:

Strategic Alliances: Partnerships with other businesses that offer complementary products or services.

Supplier Relationships: Agreements with suppliers to ensure reliable access to essential goods or services.

Joint Ventures: Collaborative projects with other companies to develop new products or enter new markets.

For example, a retailer might form a strategic alliance with a delivery service to offer convenient shipping options. A manufacturer might establish strong supplier relationships to ensure a steady supply of raw materials. Two companies might form a joint venture to pool resources and expertise for a new product development initiative. Identifying and nurturing key partnerships can:

Reduce Costs: Partnerships can help you share costs and access resources more efficiently.

Mitigate Risks: Collaboration can help you spread risks and leverage the expertise of others.

Accelerate Growth: Strategic partnerships can open up new markets, distribution channels, or customer segments.

The Power of "Who, Not How"

Ever feel overwhelmed by the thought of tackling a big project or goal all on your own? There's a powerful shift in thinking that can help: moving from "How do I solve this?" to "Who can solve this for me?"

This is the core of the "Who, Not How" principle popularized by Dan Sullivan and Dr. Benjamin Hardy. It's about recognizing that you don't have to be an expert in everything. Instead, focus on finding the right people with the right skills and expertise to help you achieve your goals. This allows you to play to your strengths, save time, and ultimately achieve greater success.

My Dinner with Beyoncé's Dad

In 2017, I attended a dinner where I met some incredibly successful people, including Mathew Knowles (Beyoncé's father) and Ken Kragen (the mastermind behind "We Are the World"). Their accomplishments are impressive, but their humility and openness about their journeys are what truly struck me.

Mathew Knowles shared how he realized early on that managing Destiny's Child required a team effort. He surrounded himself with talented individuals who complemented his skills—from producers and choreographers to marketing experts. By focusing on the "Who," he propelled the group to stardom.

Similarly, Ken Kragen emphasized the collaborative effort behind "We Are the World." He brought together diverse artists, each contributing their unique talents. This collective genius turned a simple idea into a global phenomenon.

Your "Who" Network

These stories highlight a key truth: success is rarely a solo act. Think about your own goals. Are you trying to do everything yourself? Or could you achieve more by finding the right "Whos" to support you?

Remember, building strong partnerships is about mutual benefit and respect. Be transparent about your needs, ensure fairness, and foster a long-term vision. By leveraging the power of "Who, Not How," you can tap into a world of expertise and resources, accelerating your progress and making your entrepreneurial dreams a reality.

Tony's Tiny Tacos: Feasibility in Action

Let's revisit Tony's Tiny Tacos to see how these feasibility concepts apply to a growing business. As Tony considers expanding into manufacturing and retail, he needs to assess the feasibility of this new venture.

Key Activities:

Recipe Development: Refining and standardizing the taco recipe for mass production.

Sourcing Ingredients: Establishing reliable suppliers for fresh, high-quality ingredients.

Manufacturing: Setting up a production facility and processes for mass production.

Packaging and Distribution: Designing appealing packaging and establishing distribution channels to reach retail outlets.

Marketing and Sales: Developing marketing campaigns and sales strategies to promote the taco kits to consumers.

Key Resources:

Physical Resources: Commercial kitchen, manufacturing equipment, packaging materials.

Financial Resources: Capital investment for equipment, production, and marketing.

Intellectual Resources: Tony's secret family recipe, branding, and packaging design.

Human Resources: Skilled personnel for recipe development, production, marketing, and sales.

Key Partners:

Ingredient Suppliers: Partnerships with farmers and producers for a consistent supply of high-quality ingredients.

Packaging Manufacturers: Collaboration with packaging companies to create attractive and functional packaging.

Distributors: Agreements with distributors to get the taco kits into retail stores.

Marketing Agencies: Partnerships with marketing experts to develop effective promotional campaigns.

Tony's Expansion Challenges and Opportunities

Expanding Tony's Tiny Tacos into manufacturing and retail presents both challenges and opportunities.

Challenges:

Scaling Production: Ensuring consistent quality and taste while scaling up production can be complex.

Distribution Logistics: Managing inventory, shipping, and shelf space in retail stores requires careful planning.

Marketing and Branding: Building brand awareness and differentiating the taco kits in a crowded market can be challenging.

Opportunities:

Increased Reach: Retail distribution opens up a much larger market for Tony's Tiny Tacos.

Diversified Revenue: The retail business provides an additional revenue stream, reducing reliance on the food truck.

Brand Building: Successful retail products can further enhance Tony's brand reputation and customer loyalty.

Feasibility Assessment

To determine the feasibility of Tony's expansion, he needs to carefully evaluate each of the key areas we've discussed.

Capabilities: Does Tony have the necessary skills and knowledge to manage manufacturing, distribution, and marketing? If not, can he acquire them through partnerships or hiring?

Resources: Does Tony have access to the required physical, financial, and human resources? Can he secure funding and build a capable team?

Partners: Can Tony establish strong partnerships with suppliers, distributors, and marketing experts to support his expansion?

By thoroughly assessing these factors, Tony can make informed decisions about his expansion strategy and increase his chances of success.

Tony's Tiny Tacos illustrates how assessing feasibility is crucial when expanding a business. By identifying key activities, resources, and partners, Tony can evaluate the viability of his expansion into manufacturing and retail. He can then make informed decisions about scaling production, managing distribution, and marketing his new product line effectively.

Now, let's explore how these concepts apply to your business.

Your Business Feasibility

Just like Tony, you need to carefully evaluate the feasibility of your business model. Consider the following:

Key Activities: What are the essential activities that drive your business and deliver value to customers?

Key Resources: What resources do you need to carry out these activities effectively?

Key Partners: Who can provide support and expertise to fill any gaps in your capabilities or resources?

By answering these questions and thoroughly assessing your business model's feasibility, you can identify potential roadblocks, develop mitigation strategies, and increase your chances of long-term success.

Conclusion

By carefully assessing your business model's feasibility, you can identify potential roadblocks, develop mitigation strategies, and increase your chances of long-term success. Remember, a great idea is just the starting point. Thorough planning and execution are essential to turn your vision into a sustainable and profitable business. Let's recap the key benefits of doing this work:

Increased Clarity: You'll gain a clear understanding of your business's strengths, weaknesses, opportunities, and threats.

Reduced Risk: You'll be able to identify and mitigate potential risks before they become major problems.

Improved Decision-Making: You'll have the information you need to make informed decisions about your business.

Increased Confidence: You'll be more confident in your ability to succeed.

Greater Profitability: You'll be able to set prices that cover your costs and generate a healthy profit.

Now that you've seen the benefits of assessing your business model's feasibility, are you ready to learn more about profitable pricing? In the next chapter, we'll explore strategies for setting prices that cover your costs, generate a healthy profit, and attract your target customers. Get ready to learn how to price your products or services effectively and maximize your business's profitability.

Chapter 7

PROFITABLE PRICING
Strategies for Sustainable Growth

"The single most important decision in evaluating
a business is pricing power. If you've got the power
to raise prices without losing business to a competitor, you've got a
very good business. And if you have to have
a prayer session before raising the price by 10 percent,
then you've got a terrible business."
—Warren Buffett

Pricing is a high-stakes game. Set your prices too high, and you risk alienating customers. Set them too low, and you leave money on the table. Yet, many entrepreneurs treat pricing like guesswork, relying on intuition or copying competitors. This is a recipe for disaster. In my early days as an entrepreneur, I took the industry standard approach of copying my competitors and quickly discovered it didn't work for me.

The Connection to Your Business Model

When considering pricing strategies, let's revisit the business model you started building in Chapter 4, focusing on viability. We touched on this concept when discussing revenue models, but now it's time to dive deeper. Remember, viability means your business can achieve its goals and maintain success over time. It's not just about making money; it's about ensuring your pricing strategy supports long-term sustainability and growth.

Your pricing needs to reflect the value you deliver while covering your costs. It should also consider market demand, customer willingness to pay, and your competitive positioning. A viable pricing strategy harmonizes these factors, creating a business that's both profitable and built to last.

At the beginning of this chapter, there is a quote by Warren Buffet. Think of his emphasis on pricing power. If your business model doesn't support your ability to set profitable prices, it may not be viable in the long run. That's why it's crucial to re-evaluate traditional pricing methods and ensure they align with your costs, profitability goals, and overall business strategy.

Shifting Your Pricing Mindset: Debunking Common Misconceptions

To set prices for profit, you need to address common misconceptions that can cloud your judgment. These misconceptions often stem from ingrained beliefs about pricing, and they can hinder your ability to make smart, effective decisions.

You might think pricing is all about numbers, but it's also deeply rooted in your mindset. Shifting your perspective can be the key to unlocking greater profitability.

Understanding your product or service's true value and having the confidence to price it accordingly requires a mental shift. By dispelling these myths, you can approach pricing strategically and confidently, setting prices that reflect the value you deliver.

Misconception #1: The Lowest Price Wins the Client

When setting your prices, it's easy to think that the lowest price is your golden ticket to attracting more customers.

Let's dig a bit deeper into why this might not be the best strategy for your business. Ever noticed how luxury brands rarely, if ever, compete on price? There's a good reason for that. People often equate price with quality. Offering your services or products at a price that is too low can deter your ideal customers, who might assume that cheaper equals lower quality.

Instead of offering the lowest prices, consider adopting a value-based pricing model. This approach focuses on the perceived worth of your product or service to your customers rather than just covering costs or undercutting competitors. Ask yourself the following questions: What unique benefits are you providing? How does your product enhance the lives of your customers? Once you evaluate these questions, you can price your products or services accordingly.

After you have defined your value, it is important to communicate this value clearly when reflecting it in your service. Once we have defined our value-based pricing, we'll need to look at the CVP (Client Value Proposition). The CVP, if you recall, is your marketing and sales engine that should align with the other elements of the business model and your North Star, as we discussed in our earlier chapters. Looking at pricing this way, you're not just selling services or a product but offering a valuable solution.

Once you've mastered the value-based pricing strategy as part of your growth, a scaling strategy will help you develop a price point at every level. The concept of a scaling strategy is about creating tiered pricing. It's a fantastic way to cater to different market segments without diluting your brand value. You can attract a wider audience by offering several tiers—good, better, and best—while maintaining profitability and brand integrity at each level.

Consider the clients you're attracting with your current pricing. Lower prices might bring in more customers, but are they the customers you want? Higher pricing helps filter out those who undervalue what you offer, allowing you to focus on customers who recognize and are willing to pay for quality. This shift improves your bottom line and aligns your client base with your business's vision.

This has been our experience time and time again. The client attracted to low prices is often among the most demanding clients. Often, this client interferes with your process and is hypercritical. There is an invisible line in pricing where, once you've crossed the line, the quality of your client changes drastically. The value-based client is appreciative, expressing what makes them happy. They refrain from telling you how to get the job done because, in their mind, they are paying you for your expertise.

Switching from a low-cost model to a more profitable strategy doesn't happen overnight. You'll need to prepare your customers for this change. Be transparent about why you're adjusting your prices—enhanced service quality, improved product features, or simply aligning your prices with the value you provide. This openness helps maintain customer trust and loyalty, making the transition smoother.

Your price isn't just a number. It communicates your product's value and directly influences your business's sustainability. So, step back, analyze, and align your pricing strategy with the exceptional value you offer. Your business—and your customers—will thank you for it.

Misconception #2: Competing on Price is Necessary

It's tempting to think that offering the lowest prices is the only way to win customers, especially when you see larger competitors doing so. But consider this: as a small business owner, your brand is often synonymous with you. This association gives you a unique advantage that no one else can replicate. Your superpower lies in your ability to deliver a value proposition intrinsically tied to your unique approach and personality.

Think of real estate agents. With so many realtors, why do some succeed while others struggle? Successful ones cultivate personal networks and deliver exceptional value to their clients through trust and a clear, distinctive proposition. They make the experience uniquely their own.

Or, take a look at the businesses competing for your attention on the corner outside your neighborhood. Gas stations, coffee shops, and restaurants all exist within a stone's throw of each other. They aren't competing solely on price—they thrive by offering a distinct value that speaks directly to their customer base. It could be the friendly barista who remembers your order, the gas station's consistently clean restrooms, or the restaurant's commitment to sourcing locally. Each one has a distinctive selling point that resonates with customers.

Your business can do the same. You don't have to compete on price when you're already competing on value. If you can clearly communicate your unique distinction, then truly, *you have no competition.* Your unique ability to connect, serve, and provide unparalleled value sets you apart. While others may do what you do, no one can do it how you do.

By understanding and leveraging this unique positioning, you can unlock new opportunities. Your brand becomes irreplaceable and resilient through specialization, personalized experiences, or creative pricing models like subscriptions or bundles.

Misconception #3: The Industry Standard is Always Profitable

The third misconception is believing that the industry standard is always profitable.

Here's a simple story that puts this into perspective: A husband noticed that his wife always cut off the end of a ham before putting it in the oven. Curious, he asked her why she did this. She replied that she learned to cook ham that way from her mother, but she's not sure why—it's just the way it's always been done. Wanting to get to the bottom of it, the wife then asks her mother the same question. Her mother similarly responds that she learned it from her mother. Not satisfied with the answer, they decide to ask the grandmother. When they asked the grandmother, she laughed and explained that in her day, her oven was too small to fit a whole ham, so she had to cut the end off. The reason had nothing to do with improving the taste—it was just a workaround for an old problem that no longer existed.

This is a perfect example of how outdated practices can persist. Just because a pricing model is "common" doesn't mean it's effective or right for your business today. Somewhere along the way, a business stated its pricing and everyone else followed their lead without questioning whether it was accurate or not. While industry standards can bring value to your business, you want to evaluate if the pricing is right for you before blindly adopting it.

One of our clients initially operated under Business Model #1—Low Price/Low Volume to compete with a national chain. This was a common model for her industry. As with all of our clients, when we started working together, we learned all about their business, its services, and client stories. We found that what they offered was life-changing. Clients loved them and wrote five-star reviews. The client enjoyed how they provided services and didn't want a high volume of clients. They wanted to work deeply with fewer clients. They offered personalized, impactful services that no national chain could match.

When we reviewed their pricing, we asked them to list ways their services were superior to those of their national competitor. It didn't take long for them to develop a compelling list. Then, we worked on the math.

As we broke down the math and looked at all that was being offered, the client charged 75 cents on a minute-by-minute basis, while the competitor charged $1.66 per minute. That was all the proof that the client needed to be on board with the pricing changes. The client could see the actual value they offered, and they confidently shifted to Business Model #3—High-Price, Low-Volume.

This is a common situation. Pricing is one of the tools of profitability. Yet, many business owners who need to adjust their pricing refuse to consider this tool of profitability—primarily because of money mindset and poor past experiences. Take the business owner we helped: they resisted using this tool and changing their pricing until they were shown how their services were stacked against big brands. Using a little math made all the difference and demonstrated the problem with guessing in pricing. Often, the math doesn't add up. So, remember this:

— ❧ —

**Good Business is Good Math.
If the math doesn't work,
your business won't either.**

— ❧ —

When you base your pricing on what you think the market can bear or your industry charges, you assume that your reference point is profitable. In this case, the owner assumed they were making an apples-to-apples comparison when they were making an apples-to-cabbage comparison.

How do you figure out what your pricing should be?

The answer is easy: You start with the end in mind. When working with clients on pricing strategies, we explain that determining the end has at least four components:

1. What are the expenses of the business?
2. What are the growth plans for the business?
3. What is a reasonable salary expectation for the owner?
4. What is our target net profitability?

Once we've answered these questions, then we can determine aspects that bring in balance, such as these four questions:

1. What is the sustainable amount of available work hours? (Availability)
2. What expectations do we have for a position to generate revenue? (Billability)
3. What can our resources reliably produce? (Capacity)
4. What expectations do we have to produce revenue with that capacity? (Utilization)

Step 1. Start with the End in Mind.

To begin, we determine exactly what it costs to run your business while reaching your financial goals. This isn't just about covering your immediate expenses—it includes your salary and plans for future growth. Think of it as creating a budget for the business you want to grow into, not just the business you have now.

If you already own a business, a good place to start is with your Profit and Loss Statement. Use it to learn from the past and project into the future. If you're just starting out, you might find gaps in your understanding. When we work with clients, we often see gaps in their understanding of their P&L, which we help address. That's perfectly normal. To fill those gaps, you can enlist support from your bookkeeper, CPA, and business mentors to gain a better understanding.

Once we know what it costs to run your business, we add profit to the mix. Profit standards change by industry, business stage, overhead costs, and other factors. Typically, most advisors for small and micro businesses aim for a net profit margin of around 10 percent to 20 percent. We like to challenge that status quo or industry standards.

For our service-based businesses, our goal is to achieve between 30 percent and 50 percent net profit. For our product-based business, where volume is one of the drivers, we are looking for at least 20 percent and more. If you struggle with these expectations, something may be out of alignment, but that's ok. At this moment, I am challenging you to expect more from your business, see what it is capable of, and then optimize from there.

One often overlooked aspect of pricing is how to account for owner compensation. Understanding how to factor your pay into your pricing strategy is crucial. Let's break down the three main ways you, as an owner, can get paid:

1. As the Worker with a Regular Salary
2. As the Owner with Profit Shares
3. As the Entrepreneur with the Sale of your business

First, consider a regular salary for the daily work you contribute to your business. A regular salary ensures you are consistently rewarded and sets a sustainable financial precedent for hiring someone to fill your shoes. As you grow and expand your team, shifting this budget item to a new resource is easier if your business is already paying for the work.

As the owner, you should also benefit from the business's profits. This is important on many levels because it assumes profits. Without the return of profits to you as the investor, it's like giving an interest-free donation to your job. You'd never think to do that if you worked for another company.

This is the area that allows you to build personal reserves, save for retirement, and build your own personal financial stability. If a regular paycheck is what you earn, profit sharing is what you deserve and desire.

Third, consider the long-term payoff when you eventually decide to exit the business. This is when you will see the real return on all your investment and hard work.

When we've paid the owner as a worker and as the owner, we've set you up for the long-term payoff when you decide to exit your business. A history of compensation is highly attractive to another entity or person who wants to receive a return on their investment in the business. To you, this work is your baby, and you are willing to do anything for it to survive and thrive. To a buyer, it is an investment, and they want to see how quickly they can expect a return. Of course, much more goes into successful exits—but this is a very important aspect of the preparation. The habits also create a business that is highly attractive to banks and funding sources. With this discussion, let's add owner's compensation into the math of pricing.

To see what it looks like to start with the end in mind, let's add some numbers into the components that we talked about earlier in this section and see how it looks:

1. Expenses for the Business (Overhead)		$145,000
2. Growth Plans	+	$20,000
3. Owner Salary	+	$102,080
4. Profit Margin	×	30%
Total	=	$347,204

This gives us the end goal for this part of the journey. We know from here that to meet our immediate goals, the business needs to generate $347,204 in revenue.

Step 2. Determining the Value of Your Time

Knowing what the expected revenue is for this stage of business, we can take a practical look at the work or effort it will take to make that revenue possible. Looking at this changes your quality of life. You will look at your work hours in terms of availability, billability, and utilization. We will look at the first two in this step and utilization in the next step.

Availability

This refers to the total number of hours you are willing or able to work. It's your work capacity, representing the maximum hours available to schedule and complete client projects, meetings, or tasks. Availability is a key factor in setting realistic expectations and understanding your workload limits.

Availability is how many hours you want to work and how many weeks of the year you plan on working. You may be willing to work as much as it takes to be successful, but when do you stop? What is reasonable? Since our focus is on profitability, not burning out, we focus on what is reasonable. The freedom in this choice is you are the boss. If you want to set a standard for only working four days a week in your business, you can. If you want to take the summer at half-time, you can. The only person who has the authority to tell you no is yourself.

Take a moment and look at the calendar to determine what is reasonable for you. For the sake of an example, I'll assume that you want to work 36 hours a week. You plan on taking off Christmas and New Year's, Spring Break, and want to take a two-week vacation next summer. On top of that, you have your eye on a conference that will take you out of the business for another week. That is a total of six weeks of being out of the business. With that, the math looks like this:

Hours Per Week × Available Weeks = Total Available Hours

Hours Per Week		36
Available Weeks	×	46
Total Available Hours	=	1,656

Billability

This is the proportion of available hours that can be billed to a client or project. Or the number of hours the business can earn revenue. Not all hours are necessarily billable, as activities like administrative tasks, training, and internal meetings might not be chargeable.

In truth, every hour is not a revenue-generating hour, and there should be no expectation of ever being 100 percent billable.

Remember our example of the sports instructor from Chapter 2? He had fallen into the money trap of skipping the math. When matched with revenue goals, the pricing model led to an unachievable work expectation. This is one of the areas where we can prove or disprove the math of the business.

If you are a solopreneur, I'd recommend setting a 60 percent billability target. As you develop a team, you'll have times when that can be higher. Other times, as you hire a team that can take on the roles of revenue generation and deliver on that revenue, your billability may decrease. The point is to have intention and strategy. As the team expands, we often create scenarios that can consider multiple factors, but this simple exercise can yield significant aha moments for now.

To calculate your Billable Percentage, divide the billable hours by the total available work hours. Then, multiply the result by 100 to convert it into a percentage.

Billability Percentage =
(Total Revenue Generating Hours ÷ Total Available Hours) × 100

Continuing with the exercise and assumption that you're able to bill 60 percent of your time, we see the following:

Total Available Hours		1,656
Billability	×	.60
Total Available Billable Hours	=	993.6

That gives the business 994 hours to generate revenue. If we return to our revenue goal and compare it to the available billable hours, we can determine what the business should generate on an hourly basis.

Step 3. Defining Your Hourly Effective Rate

Depending on your business model, you are going to refer to the next section of math as your revenue per hour or your hourly effective rate.

To find this number, simply divide your revenue goal by the number of available billable hours.

Hourly Effective Rate =
Revenue Goal ÷ Available Billable Hours

Revenue Goal		$347,204
Available Billable Hours	÷	994
Revenue Per Hour	=	$349.30

In this scenario, the business needs to generate $350 per hour for the available revenue hours. From here, you have choices. If you are a solopreneur, this could be your hourly effective rate to determine all project fees. If you are product-based or have other revenue-generating team members, then, collectively, this is the amount of revenue the business should be producing on an hourly basis. This is where we check the math against what is happening in the business and look at your utilization.

Utilization

This is a measure of efficiency, calculated as the percentage of available hours that are both billable and actually billed to clients. It's often expressed as a ratio or percentage. High utilization indicates that the majority of available hours are spent on profitable, client-focused work.

To figure this out for yourself, keep a timesheet for the next two weeks. Place a $ next to activities that generate revenue and add up the number of hours. Then, add up the total hours worked.

Are you or your business performing to expectations, or do you find that most of your time is spent on non-revenue-generating activities? It's a good check to perform as you walk through this exercise.

You can also impact your utilization in other ways. When it comes to invoicing the client, do you write off time or offer discounts? In some industries, this is a common and expected practice, especially in law firms. Other times, we've seen business owners lower their final invoice because the total is perceived as "large," and they worry about their clients' reactions when they see the bill.

One of the first things we do with clients is a deep dive into the numbers of the business, looking at everything we've discussed in this book so far. In our review for a client, we noticed a decline in the profitability and average sale numbers over the last three years. Discussing this finding with our client, they confided, "Some of these invoices are so large that I get worried that the client won't pay, so I discount the final amount." As we investigated the utilization of invoices, it was clear that the business had reduced a good percentage of the invoices. The impact on the business was a 5 percent loss of profits.

When we see this happen, we first suggest ending the practice and implementing a process that supports the owner in accomplishing the goal of profitability. In this case, our clients experienced a near-instant boost of 5 percent to the bottom line.

However, suppose you are in an industry where writing off time is a normal course of action. In that case, we address this issue by returning to our hourly effective rate and increasing it to compensate for the lost revenue.

Understanding your hourly effective rate can be incredibly beneficial as your business grows and evolves. It helps you identify the opportunity costs associated with spending time on lower-value tasks—essentially, work that falls outside your "zone of genius." For instance, if your effective rate is $350 per hour, it's worth considering whether you should engage in tasks that a team member could handle for $25 per hour. Even if they are slightly less efficient, delegating these tasks frees you up to focus on higher-value activities that could generate more revenue simultaneously. Why not maximize your productivity by ensuring everyone is working to their strengths?

Comparing Your Hourly Effective Rate to Your Current Pricing

Let's compare your hourly effective rate with what you currently charge for your services or products. Accurate time-tracking can prove invaluable here.

For service-based businesses: Say you charge a set fee for a project. You can determine if you're charging enough by dividing the total cost by the hours you worked on it. This tells you your earnings per hour. Is this number higher, lower, or right at your effective rate? You can also flip the calculation: divide the fee by your effective rate to see if the hours you're putting in make sense financially.

This kind of analysis works, too, for those running product-based businesses. Let's say you manufacture candles. Suppose your production line at 80 percent capacity produces 2000 units over eight hours. That's 250 units per hour. Now, look at how much money those 250 candles bring in. Is each hour of work making at least as much money as your effective hourly rate? The answer to this helps determine if your product pricing matches the effort and costs involved.

Before you decide to change your prices based on these calculations, checking some key numbers or Key Performance Indicators (KPIs) is wise. We'll cover which ones to look at later, but for now, consider how much each product costs you to make versus how much you're selling it for and how healthy your profit is on the item. These indicators will help you decide if a price change is a good move.

Pricing in Action for Tony's Tiny Tacos

To see these pricing thoughts in action, we return to Tony's Tiny Tacos Truck.

Tony's tacos were delicious, so he decided to scale his business by selling taco kits in stores. As he developed the business model for this new venture, he struggled to find the right pricing strategy.

Assumptions for Our Discussion

Cost Structure: Tony's costs include ingredients, labor, rent, and utilities.

Value Proposition: Tony's taco kits were unique and made with high-quality, locally sourced ingredients.

Customer Base: Tony's customers valued quality and were willing to pay for a premium product.

Initial Pricing Strategy and Market Analysis

Tony initially thought his taco stand pricing would translate to the new business model. After all, six tacos were six tacos, right? He set out to understand his costs and established the cost of producing a taco kit delivered to stores when manufacturing and ordering were at capacity.

Tony then looked at the landscape to see where similar products were priced. While he couldn't find direct competitors, he saw similar kits for $12 retail. Tony thought to himself, "My tacos cost more than that. Was this idea lost?"

Cost Analysis and Sales Goals

Tony and his business advisor set a goal of selling 100,000 units in the first year. They crunched the numbers to see if they could recoup the costs at a $12 price point. The analysis revealed that at $12, the business wouldn't break even until 600,000 units were sold. This could happen quickly or take a long time. Tony didn't want to take that risk. He wanted profitability sooner.

Revising the Pricing Strategy

The team went back to the drawing board to determine what it would take to make the business venture profitable sooner. They calculated that to achieve profitability at their desired scale, they would need to sell the taco kits at a retail price of $24.

Implementing Value-Based Pricing

Understanding Costs: Tony calculated his total costs, including the high-quality ingredients and the premium he paid for local produce.

Evaluating Customer Perception: He surveyed his loyal customers and found they appreciated the quality and were willing to pay more.

Setting the Right Price: Tony adjusted his prices to reflect the value of his taco kits better. Instead of pricing his kits to match similar products, he priced them based on the quality and experience he provided.

Tony's story illustrates the importance of thoroughly understanding your costs and the market landscape before setting your prices.

Whether you're offering a product or a service, pricing is a crucial component of your business model that can significantly impact your profitability and sustainability.

The Benefits of Profitable Pricing

Analyzing your pricing strategy with components like availability, billability, and utilization can unlock significant benefits for your business.

First, it helps you create a clear and sustainable pricing structure that reflects your operational realities. You'll set rates confidently, knowing where every dollar goes, ensuring you're not leaving money on the table.

With this framework, you'll gain greater financial predictability. You'll have a much clearer picture of your cash flow, giving you a better handle on managing your finances and reducing uncertainty.

You'll also identify where your time is best spent, ensuring that every hour is productive and focused on high-value tasks.

Your profitability will improve because this clarity prevents you from undercharging for your valuable services.

As a result, you'll be on a faster track to achieving your financial goals. Additionally, you'll find it easier to make strategic decisions, whether it's hiring more staff, distributing workloads, or refining your service offerings.

Clear pricing also allows for transparent communication with clients. When you understand your business math inside and out, you can confidently explain any changes in project estimates or pricing.

Lastly, this exercise lays a solid foundation for scaling your business. You'll know precisely what costs and resources it will take to reach higher revenue goals.

Ultimately, these insights will empower you to make smarter, more strategic decisions that align with your profitability goals. You'll enjoy greater financial security and the freedom to focus on what matters most in your life and business.

Navigating the Path to a Profitable Business Model

At this point, we've covered the three major segments of a business model. We began with desirability, ensuring your product or service meets market needs. Then, we moved into feasibility, examining whether your business can deliver on its promises. Finally, we worked through viability, focusing on profitability and sustainability.

You may be ready to make changes as you have worked on your business through all these thoughts.

Our next chapter will discuss implementing and managing the changes in your business. We will explore practical steps to bring your refined business model to life, ensuring you navigate the transition smoothly and effectively. Whether you are resolving friction points or gearing up to launch your new strategy, we'll provide the guidance you need to move forward confidently.

Chapter 8

MAKING CHANGES STICK
Proven Methods for
Sustainable Business Transformation

"It is not the strongest of the species that survive,
nor the most intelligent,
but the one most responsive to change."
—Charles Darwin

Change is inevitable in business, and it's something we all must face. If you're reading this, you've already made significant strides in refining your business model and understanding the importance of refining it. It's time to bring those plans to life. Darwin's words remind us that adaptability is key to survival and success. It's not enough to be smart or strong; we must be responsive to the changes around us.

At this stage in the book, you've likely identified changes that need to happen in your business. However, as the leader, implementing these changes effectively requires more than a mandate. Simply saying, "We are doing this because I said so," will fall flat with your team. You might get your way temporarily, but the changes won't last without their support. The quickest way to undo change is to lack support for it.

By learning more about change and how to manage it, the process of implementing and managing change will be more approachable and less daunting for you. We'll navigate these transitions smoothly, ensuring your business not only survives but thrives. The goal is to be decisive and committed while remaining consistent and kind throughout the process. Starting with changes in marketing and sales, we'll then move on to logistics and operations and, finally, revisit pricing strategies.

Why Lasting Change Matters

Lasting change is more important than quick fixes because it creates sustainable growth. Whether you're updating your marketing strategy, improving operations, or adjusting pricing, these changes need to stick to truly benefit your business. You'll learn how to manage them effectively so they become part of your business's new normal.

Lasting change matters because it ensures your hard work leads to long-term success and stability. It prevents the need for constant reinvention, allowing you to build on a solid foundation and grow consistently.

The Power of Effective Change Management

The power of effective change management lies in its ability to transform your organization sustainably and resiliently. It turns potential disruptions into opportunities for growth, ensuring that the changes you implement lead to lasting improvements and a stronger, more resilient business.

Why is this so important? Because business environments are always changing. Customer needs evolve, new technologies emerge, and market conditions shift. If you don't adapt, your business can quickly fall behind. But if you manage change effectively, you can stay ahead of the curve and even turn challenges into opportunities.

For example, you decide to overhaul your marketing strategy to reach your target audience better. If you plan carefully, communicate clearly with your team, execute the changes effectively, and follow up to see what's working and what's not, you're likely to see a positive impact on your business. More effective marketing can lead to increased customer engagement, higher sales, and, ultimately, more profit.

On the other hand, if changes are poorly managed, it can lead to confusion, wasted resources, and missed opportunities. Your team might be unclear about what's expected of them, leading to mistakes and frustration. This not only affects your business's performance but can also hurt team morale.

Transforming Your Business and Yourself

Effective change management can transform your business. It can lead to:

Increased Efficiency: Streamlining processes and improving operations can save time and money.

Better Customer Satisfaction: Adapting your strategies to meet customer needs can boost satisfaction and loyalty.

Higher Profitability: Effective changes can improve your bottom line by reducing costs and increasing revenue.

Mastering change management means less stress and more control for business owners. It allows them to steer their businesses confidently through transitions, knowing that they have a clear plan and the ability to adapt as needed. It also sets a positive example for their team, showing them that change can be a good thing when managed well.

Mindset Shifts: Turning Fear into Fuel for Positive Change

Most people fear change. It's a natural reaction. Change often feels disruptive and unsettling, and many of us instinctively resist it. We worry that change will lead to instability or loss, and this fear can hold us back from making necessary adjustments in our business.

Take a moment to think about the changes you've experienced in your life. Consider all the significant moments that marked a before and after on your personal timeline. Maybe it was starting at a new school, your first love, going to college, getting married, taking a memorable trip, experiencing the death of a loved one, or losing a job. These are the kinds of changes that shape our lives profoundly.

Giving Change a New Perspective

Now, let's try a simple exercise. If you list out all the significant changes in your life and put a smiley face next to the ones you view as positive and a frown face next to the ones you see as negative, what do you notice? These changes create a kind of heartbeat in your personal story, with peaks and valleys that define your journey.

Take a closer look at these changes. How many of the positive changes were initiated by your choice? How many of the negative changes were outside of your control? Often, we find that the changes we view positively are those we chose to make. In contrast, the negative changes were typically beyond our control. This pattern reveals a crucial insight: when we are the ones driving change, we tend to see it as positive. When change is forced upon us, it often feels negative.

This relationship between choice and change is key to managing and creating positive change, even in less-than-ideal situations. By taking control and making deliberate choices, you can transform potentially negative changes into opportunities for growth and improvement.

As you implement changes in your business, remember this insight. Embrace a proactive and positive approach to change. Instead of fearing disruption, see it as a chance to steer your business toward a better future. Communicate clearly with your team, involve them in the process, and encourage a culture of adaptability and resilience. When everyone is on board and understands the reasons behind the changes, you create an environment where change is accepted and welcomed.

Strategic Insights: Proven Strategies to Make Change Work for Your Business

Implementing change in your business may seem daunting, but with the right strategies, you can confidently and easily transform this opportunity into a powerful driver of growth and success. These strategies include:

Committed, but Not Attached

Being committed means you have a clear vision of where you are going and why. It's about having a strong sense of purpose and direction.

However, being committed doesn't mean being rigid. Flexibility is crucial. As you navigate the path forward, be open to how the journey unfolds. This approach allows you to adapt to new information and changing circumstances without losing sight of your ultimate goals.

Think of it like a road trip. You know your destination, but you might take different routes to get there depending on traffic, weather, or unexpected detours. This flexibility creates space for others to contribute to the transformation. Your team members can bring their ideas and insights, helping to shape the best possible path to your goals.

Decisive and Consistent: Lead with Clarity and Confidence, Like Old Faithful

Being decisive and consistent is essential when implementing change. Think of Old Faithful, the famous geyser in Yellowstone National Park. It's known for its reliable eruptions, which happen with remarkable regularity. Visitors from all over the world come to witness this natural wonder, confident that they'll see it in action. Old Faithful's predictability is what makes it so impressive and trustworthy.

As a business leader, you need to embody the same qualities. Your team needs clear direction and confidence that the decisions made are final. Ambiguity can lead to confusion and hesitancy, undermining the change process.

Make firm decisions about the changes to be made and communicate them clearly. Once a decision is made, stick to it and follow through with consistent actions. This consistency builds trust within your team, showing that you are committed to the change and that they can rely on you to lead the way. When your team knows what to expect and sees that you are resolute, they are more likely to feel secure and motivated to embrace the changes.

Stay Strategic: Know When to Pivot

However, consistency doesn't mean inflexibility. It's crucial to remain strategic and responsive to the indicators around you. If all the signs point to a need for a change in direction, don't be afraid to pivot. This doesn't mean you are being inconsistent; it means you are being smart and adaptable.

Changing for the sake of change can be just as detrimental as stubbornly staying the course for the sake of consistency. The key is to evaluate the situation carefully and make informed decisions based on data and feedback. If the current path isn't leading to the desired outcomes, reassess and adjust your strategy accordingly.

In essence, be like Old Faithful in your reliability and clarity, but also be ready to change direction when it's strategically necessary. This balanced approach will help you lead your business through change with confidence and wisdom, ensuring that you remain adaptable and resilient in the face of new challenges.

Clear and Kind

Balancing firmness with empathy is key to ensuring smooth transitions. Change can be challenging and even stressful for your team. Clear communication is crucial, but so is kindness.

One of my favorite phrases from Brené Brown's *Dare to Lead* is "Clear is Kind." It has become a personal and team mantra whenever we orchestrate transformations with our clients.

At a high level, clear and kind means that clarity in communication is one of the kindest things you can offer. When you are clear about expectations, goals, and reasons for change, you reduce anxiety and confusion. It shows respect for your team by giving them the information they need to understand and embrace the changes.

Explain the changes thoroughly, making sure everyone understands the reasons behind them and how they will benefit the business and the team. Address concerns and provide support where needed. Showing empathy and understanding can help ease anxieties and foster a positive attitude toward the change.

Imagine you're guiding someone across a bridge. You need to be firm in your instructions so they feel safe and confident but also kind and supportive, acknowledging their fears and helping them feel secure.

Combining these strategies—committed but not attached, decisive and consistent, and clear and kind—creates a powerful framework for implementing and managing change. This approach ensures that you maintain a clear vision and direction while being adaptable and considerate of your team's needs and contributions.

Action Steps: Implementing Change with Confidence

Implementing change involves a few key steps to ensure success. Let's break down each step and how you can apply it effectively in your business:

Step 1. Planning

Start by outlining what needs to change and how you will do it. This involves:

Identifying the Change: Clearly define what needs to change in your business. Be specific, whether it's a new marketing strategy, a shift in operations, or an adjustment in pricing.

Setting Objectives: Determine what you aim to achieve with this change. What are the desired outcomes? How will this change benefit your business?

Creating a Plan: Develop a detailed plan that outlines the steps needed to implement the change. Include timelines, resources required, and potential obstacles.

Step 2. Communication

Effective communication is crucial for smooth transitions. Ensure everyone on your team understands the changes and why they're happening:

Clear Messaging: Explain the change clearly and concisely. Use the "Clear is Kind" approach to ensure everyone knows what to expect.

Address Concerns: Be open to your team's questions and concerns. Provide answers and support to help them feel comfortable with the change.

Engage the Team: Involve your team in the process. Encourage their input and make them feel like part of the transformation.

Step 3. Execution

Put the plan into action and monitor progress closely:

Assign Responsibilities: Make sure everyone knows their role in the implementation process. Delegate tasks effectively to ensure smooth execution.

Monitor Progress: Keep an eye on how the change is being implemented. Track key metrics and milestones to ensure you're on track.

Adjust as Needed: Be prepared to make adjustments if things aren't going as planned. Flexibility is key to successful execution.

Step 4. Follow-up

After implementing the change, evaluate its effectiveness and make necessary adjustments:

Review Outcomes: Assess whether the change has achieved the desired outcomes. Look at the data and gather feedback from your team.

Make Adjustments: If the change isn't delivering the expected results, identify what needs to be tweaked and make those adjustments.

Celebrate Successes: Acknowledge and celebrate the successes achieved through the change. This boosts morale and reinforces the positive impact of the transformation.

How Tony's Tiny Taco Truck Communicated and Implemented Change

Tony has decided to step back from his food truck business to focus on a new manufacturing project. He needs to communicate this change to his team and hire a replacement to manage the food truck. Here's how Tony uses the framework and strategic insights to manage this transition effectively.

Planning: Tony starts by clearly identifying the change: He will be stepping back from the food truck and hiring a new manager. His objectives are to ensure the food truck continues operating smoothly and successfully launch the new manufacturing project. He creates a detailed plan outlining the steps for finding and training a new manager and how he will transition his responsibilities.

Communication: Tony gathers his team for a meeting. Using the "Clear is Kind" approach, he explains his decision to step back and why it's necessary for the growth of both the food truck and the new project. He addresses their concerns about the transition and assures them that the new manager will be well-equipped to handle the operations. Tony involves his team in the process by asking for their input on the qualities and skills needed in the new manager.

Execution: Tony assigns specific tasks to his team to help with the transition. One team member is responsible for assisting in the hiring process, while another helps train the new manager. Tony closely monitors the progress, ensuring that the new manager is integrating well and the team is adjusting to the change. He remains flexible and ready to make adjustments if needed.

Follow-up: After the new manager has taken over, Tony regularly checks in with the team to see how things are going. He reviews the performance of the food truck and gathers feedback from the team about the transition. When he notices a few minor issues, he addresses them promptly, ensuring the operations run smoothly. Tony also celebrates the team's efforts and the successful transition, reinforcing the positive impact of the change.

By following these steps and applying strategic insights, Tony effectively manages the change, ensuring a smooth transition and positioning his food truck and new manufacturing project for success.

Embrace Change with Renewed Confidence

Take a moment to reflect on the power of effective change management and the practical strategies to make lasting changes in your business.

Acknowledging the mental load of learning the "why" behind the "what" you do makes your leadership more impactful.

The good news is that once you've mastered the framework, applying it becomes second nature. Implementing change effectively won't feel burdensome but will flow naturally.

The preparation you've put into learning these concepts will reduce roadblocks and benefit your entire team. You might not even realize change is happening because it will seamlessly integrate into your daily operations. In my experience, we often refer to change as transformation because the before and after can look remarkably different.

Most of our clients initially approach us wary of change due to a lack of a solid framework or confidence in their ability to implement it. However, over the course of our first year working together, we typically see significant changes that help businesses grow and scale sustainably, improving everyone's quality of life. At that point, I encourage clients to look back on their progress and celebrate it. Universally, they are amazed by how easy and quick the transformation turned out to be, often remarking that they never imagined it could be this good.

Now that you're prepared to drive change, let's turn to practical examples of transformations in different areas of business so that you can see what you may want to implement in your own business.

Chapter 9

TRANSFORMING YOUR BUSINESS

Marketing, Operations, and Pricing

"Great companies foster a productive tension
between continuity and change."
—Jim Collins

In the realm of business transformation, Jim Collins's wisdom stands out as a beacon of guidance as he underscores the delicate balance between preserving core values and embracing necessary transformations to stay competitive and relevant. His works, such as *Good to Great*, *Great by Choice*, and *Built to Last*, highlight that true greatness is not just about making changes but about making the right changes that align with a company's enduring principles while driving it toward future success. I have naturally adopted some of his thoughts into the way I help others.

As we transition from theory to practice in this book, we'll explore actionable strategies to enhance your business's desirability, feasibility, and viability. You'll learn how to refine your marketing efforts to better align with your ideal clients, implement operational changes that boost efficiency, and adjust your pricing strategies to reflect the true value of your offerings.

By embracing the dual forces of continuity and change, you can create a business that is both robust and adaptable, ready to face the challenges and opportunities of an ever-evolving market.

Ensuring Change is in Alignment with Your Business

Before making any specific changes, it's helpful to ensure that your business model is aligned and all elements work harmoniously. A well-aligned business model supports and reinforces each part, making implementing and sustaining changes easier.

Start by examining your business model to ensure that all elements—desirability, viability, feasibility, client experience, and pricing—are aligned and support each other. The goal is to create synergy, where each part strengthens the others, making the entire system more effective and robust.

First, consider how desirability supports viability and leads to feasibility. Desirability involves understanding what customers want and need. When your products or services are attractive to your target market, this naturally leads to viability because customers are more likely to buy what you offer, ensuring revenue and profit. Viability, in turn, supports feasibility. A viable business with solid financials can invest in efficient processes and resources, making operations smoother and more manageable.

Next, think about how feasibility enhances the client experience. Efficient, well-thought-out operations lead to satisfied customers who appreciate seamless service. This positive client experience should align with your Client Value Proposition (CVP), clearly articulating the unique value your business offers.

Finally, ensure that your pricing reflects the value you deliver. Your pricing strategy should align with the perceived value of your products or services and support your overall business goals.

If you find that there isn't synergy among these elements, where the combined effect is greater than individual efforts, identifying the segments that are out of alignment becomes important. Evaluate each segment individually to identify any disconnects or areas where one element isn't supporting the others. Once you've identified the misalignments, refine these segments to bring them back into alignment, ensuring that each part of your business model works harmoniously.

When all elements of your business model are aligned, you create a strong foundation that supports successful implementation and management of changes. This alignment makes your business more resilient and enhances the overall experience for your clients and team, leading to long-term success and stability.

As you work on this, recognize that not all change is the same. Some changes are small and quick, requiring just a moment of preparation and consideration. Others are larger, unfolding in stages, and need a more comprehensive approach. When change involves people, it becomes even more crucial to manage it effectively. Taking the time to enroll and engage those impacted by the change ensures their support and makes the transition smoother. Managing people through change is vital for the change to be successful and sustainable.

Understanding these nuances will prepare you to handle various types of change with confidence and ease, leading to a more resilient and thriving business.

Making Changes in Desirability: Aligning with Your Ideal Client

Changes in desirability ensure your business aligns with your ideal client or client personas. These changes can involve adjusting who you are trying to attract, how you communicate your value proposition, or the methods you use to reach your ideal clients.

Aligning Your Marketing with Ideal Clients

Marketing changes take time to be effective. Radical changes can lead to market confusion and losing current clients. To avoid these risks, approach changes thoughtfully, allowing your new message to mature and resonate with your target audience through consistent repetition.

Financial stability is crucial during these transitions. It helps you maintain your course and find short-term income solutions to bridge the gap between your old and new messages.

Mitigating Risks and Ensuring Stability

To mitigate these risks, it's essential to approach the transition thoughtfully. The time it takes to get a new message to stick depends on several factors. Your new message needs time to mature, refine, and repeat through multiple touches. Consistency and repetition are key to making your new message resonate with your target audience.

Active vs. Passive Marketing

To master this step effectively, we recommend engaging in active marketing, which is not scalable but highly effective during times of change. Active marketing involves personal experiences, relationships, and networking. This means you or your team need to go directly to potential clients, building connections and trust one interaction at a time.

Passive marketing, on the other hand, is more scalable but less effective during initial transitions. Passive marketing includes strategies where clients come to you, such as content marketing, SEO, or through advertisements. While passive marketing is crucial for long-term growth, during a period of significant change, it's important to do the unscalable work of active marketing to ensure your new message takes hold.

Practical Steps for Active Marketing

1. **Identify Key Networks:** Focus on networking events, industry conferences, and community gatherings where your ideal clients are likely to be.
2. **Leverage Personal Relationships:** Reach out to your existing network for referrals and introductions to potential clients.
3. **Engage in Direct Outreach:** Use personalized emails, phone calls, and face-to-face meetings to connect with potential clients and communicate your new value proposition.
4. **Gather Feedback:** Use these interactions to refine your message based on real-time feedback from your target audience.

Incremental Adjustments in Desirability:
Fine-Tuning Your Focus

If your changes involve refining your message focus, targeting different industries, or exploring new channels, less risk is involved. While these adjustments may take less time, they still require a consistent effort to ensure the new message resonates with your audience.

One of the most challenging aspects of these changes is adopting a "broken record" attitude. Clients and potential clients often need consistent reminders of the change before it finally takes hold. This means you must repeat your new message frequently until it becomes familiar to your audience.

With this level of change, you are building on existing foundations rather than starting from ground zero, which can make the transition smoother and more effective.

When you align your marketing efforts with your ideal clients and focus on active marketing during transitions, you will gain traction with your new message. This approach not only mitigates risks but also helps build a strong foundation for your new marketing strategy.

Feasibility:
Making Practical Changes to Enhance Operations

Implementing major changes within your business can be daunting but rewarding. Transformations, such as introducing new technologies or restructuring teams, are designed to significantly enhance operational efficiency, improve productivity, and align business practices with long-term strategic goals.

While such changes demand careful planning, clear communication, and meticulous execution, the potential benefits can fundamentally transform your business operations. This section explores the top major changes relevant to most business owners, providing a structured approach to planning, implementing, and sustaining these critical adjustments to ensure they deliver the intended benefits.

You can apply our framework to minor and major business changes by following these steps of planning, communication, execution, and follow-up. These steps will help you effectively implement the changes and lead to positive outcomes. We will start with a minor change—revising communication protocols—and then explore a major change—restructuring the team.

A Minor Change: Revising Communication Protocols

Enhancing how your team communicates can drastically improve efficiency and reduce misunderstandings. This change involves simple adjustments that can be implemented quickly but have a lasting impact. Here's how to apply our framework:

Planning: Identify areas where communication is breaking down or could be more efficient. Choose tools or methods to streamline communication, such as introducing a team chat app or setting up regular brief meetings.

Communication: Explain the new protocols to your team, highlighting the benefits of improved communication. Ensure everyone understands how and when to use the new tools or methods.

Execution: Implement the new communication protocols immediately. Monitor the transition to ensure everyone adapts smoothly.

Follow-up: After a week or two, gather feedback from your team. Based on their input, make any necessary adjustments to further refine the communication process.

A Major Change: Restructuring Teams

Restructuring teams can help align your organizational structure with your business goals, improve collaboration, and enhance overall productivity. This change requires careful planning and sensitive handling but can lead to significant benefits. Here's how to apply our framework:

Planning: Assess your current team structure and identify areas where changes are needed. Define the new structure, roles, and responsibilities. Develop a clear plan for implementing the restructuring, including timelines and resource allocation.

Communication: Communicate the restructuring plan to your team with transparency. Explain the reasons behind the changes, the expected benefits, and how it will affect each team member. Address any concerns and provide support throughout the transition.

Execution: Implement the restructuring in phases, if possible, to allow for a smoother transition. Reassign roles and responsibilities as needed, ensuring everyone understands their new positions and expectations. Provide necessary training and support to help team members adjust to their new roles.

Follow-up: Regularly check in with your team to gauge the effectiveness of the restructuring. Collect feedback and make any necessary adjustments to ensure the new structure is working as intended. Recognize and celebrate successes to boost morale and reinforce the positive impact of the changes.

By applying our framework to both minor and major changes, you can navigate these transitions smoothly and effectively, ensuring that your business continues to thrive and grow.

Enhancing Viability:
Smart Cost Management and Strategic Pricing Adjustments

To enhance a business's viability—its ability to survive, grow, and thrive—two primary strategies often emerge: reducing costs and increasing prices.

Reducing costs is straightforward and familiar to many business owners, but it's important to be cautious. Over-cutting can starve your business, much like expecting someone to run a marathon without adequate nourishment. Approach this with a strategic eye, trimming extras but maintaining necessary expenses for growth.

Since cost reduction is a common approach, this section will focus on a major change that can significantly impact your bottom line—increasing prices.

Adjusting prices strategically requires careful planning and execution but can lead to substantial profitability improvements without sacrificing quality or customer satisfaction. We'll outline how to navigate this change effectively, ensuring your business remains competitive and continues to thrive.

Implementing Price Changes

Raising your rates may be one of the scariest things for entrepreneurs. You may worry about how your clients will react or if you lose some along the way. Plus, there's always the question: how much of an increase is reasonable?

Let's work through this together. Let's say that after reviewing your financials, you found that it's clear that it's time to adjust your pricing. Now, the question is whether to roll out this increase immediately, introduce it gradually, or some other way.

Here's something to think about: What do you think would happen if you raised your prices? Did the first concern that popped into your mind happen to be losing clients?

Honestly, raising prices will cause client attrition, but it may not impact you as much as you think. Let's break this down into something easy to digest.

- If you decide to increase your prices by 10 percent, you can afford to lose up to 9.09 percent of your clients and keep your revenue steady.
- If you go for a 50 percent price hike, you can lose a third of your clients (33.33 percent) without seeing a drop in revenue.
- Doubling your price, a 100 percent increase, means you can afford to lose up to half of your clients and still break even.
- And if you quadruple your prices, a 300 percent increase, you can lose a whopping 75 percent of your clients and not see a dip in your revenue.

This gives you a clear picture of how much leeway you have with client retention at different levels of price increases, helping you make more informed pricing decisions.

However, such significant jumps are typically not advised unless you have a solid basis and strong indicators that justify such a major change. Adjusting prices should be grounded in solid financial analysis and market research.

While the math is essential in determining the right price adjustment, your approach, preparation, and overall strategy are equally critical for success. Implementing the change smoothly involves more than just numbers; it's about managing perceptions and maintaining trust.

Determining the right amount to adjust your prices involves a calculated strategy. But implementing that change is more of an art. Let's explore how you can manage this transition smoothly, address any concerns, and find the best way to introduce your new pricing.

Overcoming the Worst Critic of a Price Change

You may encounter some resistance to a price increase. After all, you are changing expectations, and humans don't like change. However, one person is typically the worst critic of a price change.

Typically, the worst critic about increasing prices is not your client. *It is you.* You are the first person who must understand the value of your pricing and believe in it. If you aren't behind it and think it isn't valuable, you will be proven correct in the sales process. If the resistance comes from you, you need to work on shifting the statement in your head. If your first thought is, "No one will pay that," re-work the belief to "Here are three reasons people will love to pay that…" Remember our earlier example of the business owner who was undercharging and overdelivering compared to the competition? It is this step that can help overcome this hurdle.

Other business owners struggle because of their money mindset stories. In this situation, you might find yourself thinking, "I would never pay that amount." Your mind is so focused on the amount of money that the value provided for the client is irrelevant. You are suddenly making value decisions for your client that cannot logically be done.

I did this in my first business. I'm not a "stuff" person. My personal priorities are freedom, joy, and adventure. One of my favorite ways to experience these priorities is travel. In the world of interior design, it can be challenging to sell objects when you do not place importance on them. This underpinning had me less confident in presenting pricing for projects. I would spend hours worried about the invoice and finding ways to give discounts to the client so they would say yes.

While I might never spend $15,000 on a sofa, I have invested that much on a trip for my family to travel to Spain. I have easily invested that much and more into my success as an entrepreneur. I have no problem buying my clothes at Nordstrom and my groceries at Walmart. These purchases represent my values.

What I had to learn to sell those high-end products was that it wasn't about the value *I gained* from my services. It was about the value my *clients gained.* You aren't the best judge of the value gained for your client for various reasons. The biggest reason is that you are too close to the situation. This mindset shift is when selling changes from "something you do to another person" to "something you do in service of another person."

Most people will pay high dollar for quality in three categories. Those categories vary from person to person and can only be defined by that person. Stop and consider what those three categories would be for you.

Once you understand what your clients value from you, then it is helpful to rationalize how a price increase actually helps your clients.

If you are your biggest critic of a price increase or that price increase feels too big, I offer you a compromise. Set up the price increase in stages. First, determine the comfortable price increase and then go 10 percent past that. Then, after you've served three clients at that new price, adjust it again.

You can do the same for a product-based business. Your client feedback will come through your purchasing feedback, so carefully monitor them to know when you need to pivot.

How Will My Clients React?

If you raise your prices, small incremental increases are typically easier for customers to accept, especially if they are introduced gradually and with clear communication about the reasons behind them. Be prepared to communicate the WIIFM (What's In It For Me—or them—in this case). This is a vital benefit of defining your value proposition, which we will discuss in the next chapter. The positioning in place is crucial and can keep everyone happy with the change.

Go into the price increase with "Objection Busters" ready to go. To create objection busters, think of the reasons why you would get negative responses to your plan and rehearse what you would say to your clients in response to them. If you plan for them before you begin, you can often retain the client because they understand the reasons why. To include objection busters, when you share your price increases, share the reasons why you are raising your prices, and cover these objections in a positive manner.

Be willing to let people walk away. The funny thing is that your least favorite clients will likely be the first people to go. They may be fine as people; you just don't enjoy working with them. They are likely the least profitable, troublesome clients you have—let them go and bless them on their way.

Prepare for the unexpected reaction. This one most often comes from your best clients. Don't be surprised if these clients congratulate you on raising your prices or even tell you that they were surprised it took you so long to raise prices.

As your business grows, you should evaluate your pricing annually. When you grow, your expenses can increase as well. Even if your business is more established, operational expenses increase annually. Reevaluating your pricing keeps the relationship between your expenses and profits healthy.

How Should I Implement Changing My Rates?

You can say nothing and change the rate—we don't always recommend it, but it makes sense in some situations. No one likes price changes, although if you're a product-based business with a business-to-consumer sales channel, you have a greater ability to implement changes without communicating those changes.

In other situations, you need a plan grounded in your value proposition, the values of your ideal clients, and the rationale for the price increase.

The best implementation plans have a preset date in mind. This gives your clients notification of the change and time to let the change normalize in their minds.

You could also reward existing clients with the opportunity to pre-purchase at the current rate for a limited time or quantity to take advantage of the savings before the price increases. You could grandfather in previous clients and only increase pricing for new clients.

In our best plans, we have time to implement a marketing strategy that reinforces the client's value proposition before the price increase announcement.

There are so many ways to incentivize people to accept the changes. Since you know your clients best, what would they respond well to?

What Else Do I Need to Consider When Changing My Prices?

Adjusting your prices is not just about changing a number. Your marketing, sales process, and how you talk about your business also need to shift. You will want to ensure these elements align with your new pricing, helping your clients feel comfortable with the change. Your previous marketing and value propositions were tailored to your old prices. In our experience, it takes about 90 days for the effects of new marketing efforts to fully take hold. During this time, you might find more people saying "no'" than usual. This signals that your sales process may need some adjustments to support your new pricing strategy better.

Don't be discouraged by this process. It's an excellent learning opportunity. Paying attention to client feedback during this period can provide valuable insights, enabling you to make informed improvements. This way, you're not just guessing what works but actively refining your approach to better meet customer needs.

Price Increases in Action:
Transforming Challenges into Opportunities

Let's explore three compelling case studies that illustrate how strategic price increases can lead to remarkable business growth and customer loyalty. Each example showcases a different scenario, from incentivizing long-term contracts to enhancing the owner's quality of life, providing you with practical insights and inspiration for your own pricing strategy. Let's see how these businesses approached the challenge, managed customer expectations, and secured their market position through well-planned price adjustments.

Case Study #1: Leveraging Community and Value

One of our Profitable Growth Incubator clients knew they needed to raise prices. The previous year, every client moved from month-to-month contracts to annual contracts paid monthly. The move worried the business owner, so they dropped their rates to incentivize clients to sign up. Everyone took up the offer gladly, and the business lost $10,000 in revenue every month for the year. A few months later, the unintended consequences were beginning to take their toll.

In preparation for raising prices, we followed our change framework: planning, communication, execution, and follow-up. We started by looking at the KPIs, conducting a competitive analysis, and discussing our options for the price increase. One of the indicators that stood out was conversion—the ability of a lead to convert to a client—and retention—the percentage of clients that stayed multiple years. We sensed an opportunity but investigated further. Both KPIs were outperforming the industry—why?

The answer was in their value proposition. The clients were looking for the service but stayed for the community. They said yes because they felt unconditionally accepted.

Planning

Understanding that there was such high value recognized, we implemented a multi-faceted plan. First, we decided to raise prices for new clients immediately. The new prices were on the high side of average, but not overly so. We didn't expect too many price objections, especially if the reason they bought was reinforced.

Communication

We openly communicated the new prices to existing clients, but it did not impact them because of their existing contracts. For the next three months, we enhanced the normal community-building efforts of the business but also improved how they were marketed and shared with the community. The aim was to reinforce the reason the clients continued to purchase.

Execution

We launched the communication plan for existing clients three months before contracts were ready to renew. We informed them of the new terms and the reasoning behind the increase. Finally, our client spoke with all 111 of the existing clients personally.

Follow-up

Guess how many people did not renew? One. And that one person was moving away, so they would not have renewed even if the prices had stayed the same.

This was one of the more extensive plans for a client and a significant increase in pricing. Oftentimes, the implementation is a simpler and more straightforward process. In these cases, the framework may not be needed.

Case Study #2 Raising Prices Immediately to Fuel Rapid Growth

Another client raised their rates after years of being priced under the market. Their confidence in the value they were providing was strong enough that they could explain the increase confidently. This company chose to implement the price increase immediately. In the process, they lost two customers. On the one hand, they were sad because they enjoyed the clients as people. However, the work was out of alignment with where the company had evolved. Ultimately, the increase fueled a new period of rapid growth in revenue and profits.

Case Study #3 Increasing Freedom

A third client elected to raise prices to improve the owner's quality of life. At their current prices, they were swamped. While a few previous clients did not renew, most new clients did not worry about the prices. The price increase provided freedom for the owner, allowing the business to serve fewer clients and work fewer hours while revenue and profit grew.

Ultimately, if a price change makes sense mathematically, it is time for the strategies and mindset to align and look at the correct method of raising prices. However, your true value will often solidify loyalty, attracting clients who appreciate what you do and are willing to pay for quality.

How will you handle a price change?

As you consider your next steps, remember that effective communication is important. Clearly explain the reasons behind your price adjustments to your clients. Highlight enhancements in services, improvements in quality, or increases in operational costs. Clients who understand the value they're receiving are more likely to remain supportive, even at higher price points.

Encourage yourself to view price increases not as a barrier but as an opportunity for growth. This is your chance to elevate your business, reinvest in your offerings, and ultimately deliver even better service. With the right mindset and strategy, your business can thrive with a price increase.

So, take a deep breath and step forward with confidence. You've done the math and seen the case studies—now it's time to act. Raising your prices is a strategic move that reflects the growing value of your business. Trust in the quality of your offerings and the loyalty of your clients as you use this opportunity to take your business to the next level.

If all the indicators say that now is the time to change your pricing so that the math of the business works, then you are ready for our next chapter on crafting a profitable client value proposition. This message will aid you as you make changes to the financial parts of the business. It also adds depth to your North Star, by helping you clearly communicate who you work best with, why, and to what extent.

Conclusion: Embracing Change for Growth

Before we move on, let's revisit the broader concept that has guided our discussion. Embracing change, while often uncomfortable, is where true growth and progress happen. Jim Collins's quote at the beginning of this chapter reminds us that maintaining a productive tension between continuity and change is crucial for fostering a thriving business.

To give your mind a brief respite, let's focus on a small, actionable step you can take today. Identify one minor change that you can implement in your business. It could be revising your communication protocols, refining your marketing message, or adjusting your pricing strategy. Use the framework and examples provided in this chapter to guide your next steps.

Take a moment now to reflect on one small change you can make. Write it down, plan it out, communicate it clearly, execute it diligently, and follow up to ensure it sticks. Embrace the process and watch as these small changes lead to significant progress and growth for your business.

Remember, the goal is not to overhaul everything at once but to make incremental changes that accumulate over time. You will build a more adaptable, resilient, and successful business by consistently applying these principles.

Chapter 10

MASTERING GROWTH MOMENTUM
Strategic Foundations
for Predictable Returns

"True mastery, it turns out, is not found in accumulating each and every tool under the sun. True mastery is learning that there are really only a handful of tools, and it is the proper application with correct timing and setting that makes them so useful."
—Chris Matakas,
My Mastery: Continued Education Through Jiu Jitsu

Getting overwhelmed by shiny new tools and strategies is easy in business. Something new promises to be "the ultimate solution" to all your problems every day. But real growth isn't about hoarding tools or trying to use everything. It's about mastering and applying a few core strategies at the right moments.

Think of it this way: a master chef doesn't rely on every spice in the kitchen, and a skilled carpenter doesn't need every tool in the toolbox for each job. Instead, they know what works best and when to use it for optimal results.

As a business owner, it's about understanding what's truly essential to your unique business journey and mastering those tools, whether it's refining your marketing approach, improving customer experience, or managing your finances efficiently. When you deeply understand a handful of key strategies, you become confident in precisely timing their application. This approach can transform your business into something resilient and powerful, like a well-trained jiu-jitsu master who's learned that winning isn't about trying every move but timing the right ones. This understanding of what's truly essential gives your business a sense of purpose and strategic direction. To develop this skill, though, we need to better understand the nature and characteristics of growth.

Growth's Secret: Harnessing the Unseen

I like to remind myself that growth is fickle. It's the phrase I whisper to myself when the growth plan was supposed to go right, and growth decided to go left. *Fickle* means changing frequently, especially regarding one's loyalties, interests, and affection. Growth feels that way. It is not stagnant. It needs to be cajoled and coaxed into reality. It can be equally thrilling and challenging and requires constant attention.

When you decide to start growing, it can be challenging because it takes momentum.

To explain *momentum* easily, let me share a story. I had friends back in high school who would invariably run out of gas. They would try to start pushing the car on their own, but it would not budge. However, if a couple of us would hop out of our vehicles and help push their car, it would start moving. Someone could push it by themselves after it got rolling. That is momentum. Momentum is simply strength or force gained by motion or a series of events. Our friend, Jim Collins, explains this concept as a Flywheel Effect in *Good to Great*. The beginning is tough and requires constant attention. Then you reach a tipping moment where momentum takes over and carries you forward.

Growth needs momentum to work. Growth is one of the hardest things to create in a business, but it is also one of the easiest to keep going—as long as it goes in your desired direction. That's an important distinction because momentum is neutral. It can cause your business to spiral upwards toward greater and greater success or go the opposite way toward more and more problems. Feedback loops and compound effects keep the momentum flowing in the direction of energy.

We will continue to discuss these two ideas in more detail. For now, think of feedback loops as a cycle where the results of your actions are looped back to influence those actions again, making the effects stronger or more consistent over time. Compound effects are like a snowball rolling downhill. Small actions that might seem insignificant at first can add up, creating big changes after a while.

In business, we see how energy and momentum show up. If the growth momentum and compound effects are good, that's great! You grow easily and sustainably. If the momentum is good, but the compounding effects are negative, it feels like you are battling the growth and lurching along. Even more frustrating is when the idea falls flat. There is no momentum and no growth. It looked good on paper but did not pan out as you planned.

Growth is also fickle because it doesn't always act as we think it should or as it has in the past. *What worked today likely will not work tomorrow.*

The rapid rate of change in our world means we must pay attention to our intuition when things feel off. The feedback loops we've built into our business help us make shifts sooner rather than later.

The key here is knowing when to keep with strategy and when to abandon it. That is more of an art than science. Some feedback loops we put into place are fast and easy to see, such as declining profitability. Others, like name recognition, are slower to catch over time. How you manage those will determine the impact of a strategy on your business.

We know we need feedback loops, information, and data to let us know whether we are on track or off track. However, many businesses are not using feedback loops to drive their business. They consistently react to everything that comes their way and always feel surprised by what happens in their business.

The lack of using these feedback loops and the inability to understand its nuanced behavior is why a "Hail Mary" maneuver—a move that a business owner hopes will save the day—has a 50/50 chance of saving a business. A move that a business owner hopes will save the day. However, the move may not be big or fast enough to stop the downward spiral, especially if you've waited too long. In my experience, waiting too long to change only accelerates the downward spiral.

Why do entrepreneurs wait too long to change a growth strategy that isn't working? They get attached to the path they've designed for themselves, and routine and comfort work against them. Positive qualities, such as hope and belief, can also work against change.

Yet change is growth. By its very definition, if your business stays the same, you are likely not growing. If your business is not growing, you will experience a slow loss of momentum that may take a long time to see. When you finally see it, it may be too late. You will feel like you are starting all over, working hard to regain growth momentum.

Mastering Compounding Effects

We also must consider the compounding effects. Managing these is as nuanced as managing the feedback loops.

The idea behind the *compound effect* is that small changes repeated over time generate significant changes.

Darrin Hardy, publisher of *Success Magazine* and author of *The Compound Effect: Jumpstart Your Income, Your Life, Your Success*, shares the relationship between hamburgers and heart attacks to explain the compound effect. The simple act of eating a hamburger will not cause a heart attack. It is the daily action of eating hamburgers that increases the likelihood of a heart attack.

On the flip side, Dave Ramsey shares the story of compounding interest. Jack invests $200 for nine years from ages 21-30, then stops. Blake invests $200 from ages 30-68 (38 years). At 68, who should have more money? Based on compound interest calculations, Jack has $2.35M, and Blake has only $1.3M. He invested $69,600 more but never caught up.

The deceptive aspect of the compound effect is that, initially, you don't see any noticeable changes, so it appears harmless. When repeated daily, positive actions don't seem to make a difference in the short term. Once they reach the tipping point, that change is noticeable. Now, think about your business—where is the compound effect working for or against you? Is it with your team, your clients, or your cash flow? Do you have a back-of-the-neck feeling about one of these areas but can't pinpoint it?

I will talk more about feedback loops and compound effects in the next chapter. But, to use them fully, you need to deeply understand growth. Let's start by looking at the foundations that are needed in your business to be able to grow strategically.

Building Your Business on Solid Foundations

If you want to grow and scale your company, you need these seven foundations in place. When you look to solve a problem and meet your company's potential, your growth plan will need resources from these foundations.

These seven foundations include:

1. Sales
2. Marketing
3. Time Management
4. Cash Flow Management
5. Team Leverage and Development
6. Process and System Creation
7. Pricing and Profit Planning

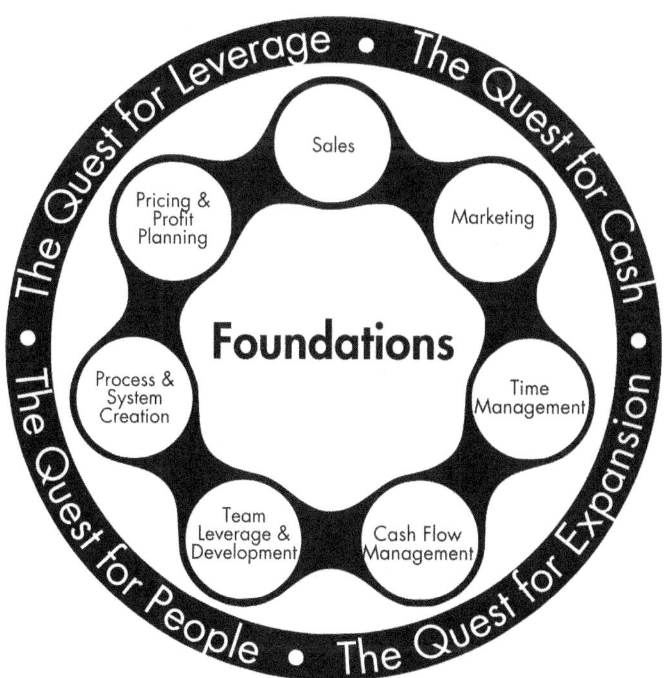

Business Growth Occurs in Stages

When you begin your business, you enter the infant and toddler stage, where you develop a core ability to build your foundations. This stage is typically about proof of concept. Do people need and want what you are selling? Are they willing to pay? Can you deliver? These are the basics of how you can function as a business. As a toddler, you progress further, learn to walk, and maybe even run. Your business develops a personality, and it begins to test its limits. You quickly learn what rules need to function better, where you need improvement, and what isn't working.

Enter the teenage stage, your business develops further, and the need for people and a community around your business emerges. You find greater demands on your time. Things that once felt sustainable are pushing you to the limits. Your independence says you can do it all on your own, yet that creates struggle.

The teenage years of a business are like its growth stage. During this time, establishing the seven key foundations is crucial. These foundations prepare the business for the next stage: scalability.

Eventually, your business will mature into the adult stage, where you're more proficient at being an entrepreneur and managing the phases of growth, scalability, and recovery. Your business may even experience a midlife crisis along the way. Understanding this journey is the basis of the study of the lifecycle of an organization. If we plotted on a graph, it would look like a capital S tilting forward. Being aware of the organizational life cycle helps guide your business through these stages well and will set you up to choose how and when to exit your business. Understanding makes it easier to align your expectations with where your business currently stands.

As you navigate this path, fundamental truths about growth are necessary to grasp. Understanding these truths will help you pinpoint exactly where you are and determine the next best steps for your business.

Growth is Sequential and Necessary

The development of your business has a sequence, and while the sequence isn't time-bound, it can't be skipped. Let's go back to our infant/toddler analogy. Would you expect a toddler to go from crawling to running and winning a marathon without learning to walk first? While every toddler has their own timeline for the process, they all hit the sequence of crawling, standing, and walking. That journey, from baby to baby, is so personalized. My older son went through the phase rapidly, walking at 10 months. Our second son started walking at 15 months. Was one journey better than the other? Not at all. Did their journeys influence each other? Most definitely, our younger son had less desire to walk because he could get his brother to bring him what he wanted.

In life, you would have no expectations of the process, only a couple of indicators that milestones weren't met within a time range, a form of a feedback loop.

The same concept applies to business growth; it's about measuring the progress of milestones.

We use the term quest to describe business milestones. Every business goes through these aspects of business development to reach the next level of success.

Four Quests for Business Growth

The four "quests" that business owners seek to support the development of their foundations typically happen in the following order:

1. Quest for Cash
2. Quest for Leverage
3. Quest for People
4. Quest for Expansion

If your proof of concept is failing and your ability to attract and retain clients is rocky, then you are likely on the Quest for Cash. Your foundation focus should be on marketing, sales, and perhaps pricing.

If your business is full of clients, but you are killing yourself and have nothing to show for it, then you are adding the Quest for Leverage (doing more with what you have) to your Quest for Cash. The foundations of time management and process can be paired with pricing, profit planning, and cash-flow management.

If you struggle to deliver a consistent product or service to your client, perhaps process and system creation or time management is a focus, or the business model is off.

Then, there's team leverage and development, the ability to build an engaged team to help carry your business forward. Installing these key members is a foundation of growth that ensures the business can grow beyond your efforts.

Once these three quests are completed, then it's time to think about expansion through growth or scalability.

Growth is Iterative

While your business can mature from infant to teenager, to adult, and then into retirement, it's important to realize that success in business through its maturation is not a linear progression. This means you are never really done. Instead of treating growth as something you accomplish once and then move on, growth in your business is iterative, more like a spiral.

With this spiral, you can always go up, and you can always go down. You might hit a landing (a plateau) or an invisible glass ceiling along the way. You can take two steps at a time or sprint up. Or, you might also have creaking knees and be arduous and slow.

Envision what will happen to growth if your business is this spiral staircase. As you grow, you should be able to reap a few benefits along the way—increased cash through better pricing, which, in turn, invites an elevated client, which allows you to do better work, which gives your clients better results, which, in turn, enables you to charge for the value of your work. This is momentum at work for you.

As you grow your cash and profits, you can make more investments to increase your personal workload and get out of the "chief cook" and "bottle washer" roles. You invest in technology that makes the work more efficient, easier to communicate, and easier to see documentation, which, in turn, allows you and your staff to do more with less. Growth has its own pace, and your impatience will not speed it up. That's just the nature of growth.

Instead, if we see growth as a consistent building of momentum with a sequence, we only need to keep taking the next step to achieve our goals. This becomes easier when you can move from "pushing" growth to "allowing" growth. It's a process that builds over time and can be sustained by its momentum.

In practice, the building of momentum can be incredibly frustrating. Entrepreneurs find themselves forever locked into a constant state of achieving great things and seeing opportunities for even more greatness—a duality of business of achievement and things needing to be refined. When you've put a great foundation in place, you will find ways to improve it. As you find ways to leverage your business to do more with what you have, you switch adventures to go on the Quest for Cash to become more efficient.

I suggest viewing your time as an entrepreneur as a journey. The journey includes improving your entrepreneurial skills, facing a variety of new challenges every day, and experiencing success along the way instead of attaching it to "someday when."

Growth is an Investment

It will always take some sort of investment before you see growth. This could be an investment in people, time, or money.

One of the definitions we like the most that helps business owners understand the investment is that growth is defined as investing one dollar and receiving nearly one dollar in return over time. Scaling, however, is about exponential returns, where the expectation is that the dollar of investment returns exponentially and often faster than growth. If growth is a spiral staircase, scaling is a rocket.

The problem is that growth devours cash. You may wonder how you will pay for it as you enter a growth period. You can seek funding—but most small and micro businesses aren't attractive to traditional funding sources. Don't fret. This is the case for a large percentage of the businesses we work with. It only means we must get crafty and self-fund our own growth.

To self-fund growth, I typically have my clients find the money in two ways. The first prepares for the future by setting aside money for growth in the second tier of the profit plan. The second is quicker, as we look for more immediate cash by taking advantage of low-hanging opportunities to activate the money for investment.

You have a low-hanging opportunity now where you can easily achieve 10 percent growth. Are you prepared for what it is? The answer is: *Pay attention to your business.* I know you are paying attention to your business. But, I want you to choose one aspect of your business that, if improved, would have an impact. Then, set an improvement goal and create a feedback loop or key performance indicator to track it. Put the tracking information somewhere visible so everyone can see it and watch what happens.

Here's the science behind this move. When you increase your awareness and pay attention, your conscious and subconscious go into hyperdrive.

Making little adjustments will be easier when the subconscious is working on making your goals come true. You will have those "aha" moments in the shower or doing other mundane tasks when your brain can see the solution by documenting and being intentional about what you want.

Successfully growing your business takes more than just a spur-of-the-moment decision. It can start with a thought. For it to be successful, the thought requires careful planning, monitoring feedback loops, and smart use of your resources. By setting achievable goals and clear measures for tracking progress, you can make steady improvements that lay a strong foundation for eventually expanding your business more aggressively. Be deliberate about where you invest your efforts, ensuring each step helps build lasting growth.

Instead of viewing growth as something happening to you, consider it a strategic decision—a conscious choice you make to shape your business's future. This new way of thinking about growth as proactive, not reactive, can change how you drive your business forward.

Growth is a Strategy

Growth shouldn't surprise you. When I hear people speak of growth as a surprise, it usually is right before they talk about one of the most challenging periods in the business because they were not ready for the growth and did not have strategic foundations in place.

I once read that a study of Fortune 500 businesses found that companies that experienced the highest growth years often file bankruptcy 18 months later. That's what growth as a surprise can do to a business. And it happens to small businesses.

At an event I attended, a panel of business owners shared their growth experiences. One owner shared that they were surprised their business had grown 287 percent in six months. This increase in business required more team, technology, and investments to sustain. The stress was so intense that the business was on the brink of shutting down. The owner turned to banks for financial help, but the applications were declined because the cash position was poor. The business owner had no choice but to scale back, laying off a portion of the team to recover. From the owner's perspective, the story's moral is to be wary of rapid growth and pay close attention to your business. I disagree with the first part and agree with the second part. Let me paint you a different way to look at this story.

Instead of reacting to growth, imagine how treating growth as a strategy could have played out for the owner. If we had been involved in the story, it would have sounded more like this: Using the business's KPIs and feedback loops, the owner could see that their services' demands were picking up rapidly.

We analyzed the data and determined that the business could grow by 250–300 percent in six months. Working together, we asked if we grew that fast, what in the business would break, and what would the business require regarding resources? We identified that the client's onboarding process represented a bottleneck with the rapid pace of growth. We decided to overhaul the workflow, automate where possible, and systematize the rest.

We looked at the team's capacity and estimated that while the team had the capacity to take on more, we would likely need to hire two months into the growth plan and again at four months. Even with the extra hands, we could still see places where the process and growth could become more efficient.

Once we knew the investment needed to fuel the growth, we plugged the numbers into our predictive cash flow tool. The investments at two months would significantly drop profits, but it was sustainable. It was the investments at four months that would drain the business of cash. We would recover from those expenses after five more months, but we might need $50,000 to cover operational expenses. After this point, though, things looked much better as the business realized the cash from the growth. While a drain, the business has a plan to pay back the $50,000 in the next five months.

Armed with this knowledge, we could bring the profit plan to the strategic discussion. Did we have a combination of $50,000 in reserves, profit buckets, and tax savings from the loss to offset the investment? Maybe yes, maybe no. What is more common is that we have much of the money needed and only need to make up a smaller remaining balance. The point is that we have a choice. Since there is money in the bank, we could go to a bank and get an operating line of credit. We could receive payments on outstanding invoices, tighten up payment terms inbound, or seek terms for outbound payments. We could craft a quick-turn product or service to generate the cash needed. In the end, the business would be able to ride the flow of growth.

If you view growth as a strategy, you make better decisions. Better decisions have better results.

All growth has inherent risks. Once you've mastered the strategic approach to growth, you can take things to the next level by layering your growth strategies as a defensive, protective strategy in the business.

Growth is about Generating Reliable Returns

Imagine your business growth strategies as seeds planted in the fertile soil of opportunity. You want a continuous harvest, not all at once.

Let's consider my favorite vegetable, green beans. My husband, "Farmer Ed," knows this and plants various green beans to enjoy: Jade, Contenders, and the delectable Roma. Each variety has its timing, so I can enjoy fresh green beans across a more extended season. Ed pays attention to the "days to maturity" information—the number of days before a plant begins to yield fruit. This way, I get the most beans for the longest period.

Last spring, amidst the whirlwind of our older son's senior year and his final high school baseball season, we barely had time to tend to our garden. During the first brief respite, I checked on our bean plants. To my dismay, they had reached the end of their lifespan, taking the last harvest of untouched beans with them.

I could have extended their lifespan with better care and enjoyed an even more bountiful harvest. When picked at the perfect moment, green beans are at their peak—plump with goodness from the mother plant. Wait too long, and they become fibrous, losing their appeal. Leave the fruit on the plant and it can drain the plant of energy to create more fruit.

Now, think about your small business and your growth goals. The same principle applies. When we force results on our timeline, we often need to remember that time is, in many ways, irrelevant. Strategies will take the time they need to mature, just like those green beans.

The thought process of layering your growth strategies to give you a more extended season makes good sense. We simply need to pay attention to the "days to maturity" for each strategy.

We categorize every strategy that makes it to the strategic plan based on expected returns, or "days to maturity," into one of these four categories:

1. **Quick Wins:** Generate a result in 30 days or less
2. **Short Term:** Generates a result in 90 days or less
3. **Medium Term:** Generates a result in 90–180 days
4. **Long Term:** Generates a result in 180+ days

The estimated time to generate a result should include the time to develop and implement the strategy and the time it takes to deliver results. Have you considered evaluating the growth strategies you choose for your business in this way? Where would the bulk of your strategies fall if you were to categorize all that you do strategically?

Understanding how long a strategy will take to produce results and when to layer in each approach to see returns today, tomorrow, and next year can be challenging. That's why we provide clients with a comprehensive tool listing our 169 strategies and a guideline for their expected timing. This helps business owners feel confident in their decisions, knowing they can plan strategically and maximize their growth potential.

Commonly, after categorizing the strategies, most business owners find that their efforts are in the long-term category when they need short-term results. This approach is like putting all your eggs into one basket. The lack of diversity puts all the pressure on a long-term strategy to produce while creating or amplifying problems in the short term.

Instead, we recommend that business owners align the timing of these strategies to the business's cash needs. The stronger the need for cash, the more emphasis on shorter-term strategies. The more cash-stable the business is, the more long-term strategy can come into play. Each quarter, we want to see at least one quick, short, and medium win strategy so the business can realize reliable returns throughout the year to give the business a more diversified approach. If one strategy fails, it's not going to capsize the business.

As we've explored, growth isn't just about expansion but strategically navigating the ebbs and flows that come with it. It's about pushing past initial inertia—much like helping a friend push-start a car—and then maintaining the momentum to keep moving forward.

What About Your Business?

As we conclude this chapter on the dynamic nature of growth and the necessity of momentum, take a moment to reflect on how these concepts play out in your business strategies:

Reflect on Momentum

Think about a recent time when your business experienced a surge in growth. What initiated it? How did you and your team respond? Did you manage to sustain that growth, or did it taper off? Reflecting on these questions can help you understand the nature of momentum in your business.

Evaluate Your Current Strategies

Are your strategies reactive or proactive? Just as we discussed the dangers of being caught off-guard by growth, assessing whether your business is merely reacting to changes or strategically planning for growth is essential.

Prepare for Strategic Decision-Making

In the upcoming chapter, we'll explore how Key Performance Indicators (KPIs) and feedback loops are not just measurement tools but vital components of your strategic toolkit. These tools help you maintain growth momentum by providing real-time data, enabling you to make informed decisions swiftly.

We will ensure your growth is maintained and accelerated by exploring how to turn these insights into actionable strategies. Prepare to dive deeper into how these tools can transform your approach to business strategy, turning potential challenges into opportunities for sustainable development.

Chapter 11

GROWTH GPS
Turning Data
into Actionable Strategies

"It is a capital mistake to theorize before one has data. Insensibly,
one begins to twist facts to suit theories,
instead of theories to suit facts."
—Arthur Conan Doyle,
"Sherlock Homes: A Scandal in Bohemia"

Think about your business like a road trip. You've got a map laid out, and you know your destination. But along the way, unexpected things can pop up—like a scenic detour you want to explore or road construction forcing a change of route. New opportunities and challenges will keep emerging, making you rethink your original plans. This is where the strategic value of key performance indicators (KPIs) and feedback loops comes into play.

KPIs are like GPS, showing whether you're on track or need to adjust your course. The feedback loops help you quickly recognize shifts in the market, customer needs, or your business environment so you can adapt your plans before veering too far off course.

By regularly checking these "road signs," you can stay agile and responsive, adjusting your strategy to reach your business goals even as the journey changes. The road might have twists and turns, but you'll be better equipped to navigate toward success with KPIs and feedback loops guiding you.

How much growth is good growth?

As business strategists, we believe every growth percentage—from the smallest to the largest—should be celebrated. In the previous chapter's story of the business owner, it is easy to see why exponential growth can be scary, especially if you are unprepared. What if, though, it was intentional?

As you have been reading, are you intrigued by how to achieve it for yourself? I hope so because we'd like to show you how in this chapter.

We find that exponential growth is totally possible for our clients. We know how to make it happen when we establish KPIs. When you determine these for your business and put in the foundations we've outlined in this book, you'll see how easy it can be.

It often takes the same effort and time to grow 10 percent as it does to grow 100 percent, so why not go for it?

A Primer to Key Performance Indicators

Before we discuss the seven essential KPIs that drive a growth feedback loop, let's consider some basic thoughts and definitions.

Key Performance Indicators or KPIs are measurable values (or data) that demonstrate how effectively a company achieves its goals. Within the business, we have a lot of data, often numerical. For instance, *measuring* how many new clients you worked with this month is easy, but you need more context for the measure's performance with that data point alone.

Metrics are comparisons of measures with other relevant measures or over a period. For instance, if you tracked your leads (a measure) and your new clients (a measure) for the same period, you could create a metric of conversion (new clients ÷ leads). Let's say you had 35 leads and 10 new clients last month. You could calculate your conversion rate:

$$\textbf{\textit{New Clients} ÷ \textit{Leads} = \textit{Conversion Rate}}$$
$$\textbf{\textit{10 Clients} ÷ \textit{35 Leads} = 28.6\%}$$

The **Conversion Rate** gives a relationship to monitor, but it still doesn't tell us if the resulting 28.6 percent is on-track or off-track. We need more of a frame of reference.

Now, imagine that you've looked at the history of this metric, and over the last three years, your business has performed at 65 percent conversion.

Suddenly, the context tells you that something is off, especially if the key performance indicator you've set as the goal is 65 percent or better.

KPIs are most effective when they are specific, relevant to business goals, realistic, attainable, time-bound, and measurable.

There Are Also Different Types of KPIs

1. **Quantitative:** measurable and expressed in numbers, like total income, profit margin, and customer acquisition costs.
2. **Qualitative:** measurable through subjective assessments, like customer satisfaction and net promoter score.
3. **Leading:** these predict future performance and can indicate what might happen, such as the number of sign-ups for a new product.
4. **Lagging:** these reflect success or failure after an activity is completed and reflect what did happen.

What Tony's Doctor Told Him

As Tony has been working on his tiny tacos, apparently, he ate too many of them. His doctor has advised him to lose weight to feel better and lower his blood pressure. So, how do we look at the KPIs for this?

1. **Quantitative Example** (measurable and expressed in numbers): Pounds lost.

   Explanation: This is a straightforward, measurable figure that indicates exactly how much weight has been lost. It's a clear numeric value that can be tracked over time. If Tony's goal weight is 225 pounds, this is one of his KPIs. It can be measured and compared. He can regularly weigh himself and record his weight loss to measure his progress.

2. **Qualitative Example** (measurable in subjective ways): Improved feelings of well-being and self-esteem.

Explanation: Unlike pounds lost, this isn't a number you can easily measure, but it's a significant indicator of success in a weight loss journey. You might assess this through self-reported surveys or journals in which the individual notes how they feel physically and mentally as they progress.

3. **Leading Examples** (Items changed almost instantly): Consistency in daily physical activity, tracking what type of food is eaten, and how much.

   Explanation: This KPI predicts future weight loss success and is a good indicator of behavior change. By tracking how consistently someone engages in physical activity, you can understand their commitment and likelihood of achieving their weight loss goals.

4. **Lagging Example** (These items show something you cannot choose to change but are changed because of something else): Actual weight loss measured after a specified period.

   Explanation: This KPI assesses the outcome of diet and exercise efforts after they have occurred. It confirms whether the strategies implemented have been effective in achieving weight loss.

Here are the similarities between Tony's story and your business. Before change, it's beneficial to establish a baseline for your KPIs. This lets you know where you've been. With the baseline in mind and what we know about your vision, the market, and the business, we choose the goal. It lets us know where we are going. Then, we look at the leading and lagging indicators.

Leading indicators are the ones we can put strategies in place to impact. Lagging indicators are the result of the leading indicators. We don't change them; they simply are what they are.

Leading indicators are tracked more frequently, while lagging indicators show improvement over a longer time, so there is a longer cadence between tracking.

You can go a little crazy tracking the business—that isn't the goal. We are looking for simplicity, to track the fewest, because that is sustainable. These few create a dashboard that indicates whether the business is on track to meet its goals or off track. Our most frequent cadence is to review our KPIs monthly, within 15 days of the close of the month. Then, we review the trends quarterly and annually to drive strategy.

With a baseline of indicators, let's examine the top seven and the power they give you to choose your growth strategy.

These foundational KPIs are primarily quantitative and are comprised of both leading and lagging indicators. KPIs are crucial because they provide a focus for strategic and operational improvement, create an informed basis for decision-making, and help focus attention on what matters most. Managing KPIs often means improving leading indicators that later drive lagging indicators.

KPIs are meant to be seen front and center. This can create positive tension for you and your team. As they see the changes that the business plans on making, it provides clarity of focus, and as we mentioned, their awareness alone can yield 10 percent growth.

Essential KPIs to Monitor for Growth

Together, these numbers and your financial statements provide a comprehensive dashboard that can guide strategic decisions from marketing to financial planning.

They can help you enhance growth and profitability in real time, adjusting your strategies promptly in response to any signs of growth or decline, ensuring your business remains on a successful trajectory. The seven essential metrics to monitor for growth are:

1. Leads
2. Conversions
3. Average Sale in Dollars
4. Average Number of Purchases per Client for a period
5. Gross and Net Profit in percentage
6. Cost of Acquisition (COA)
7. Lifetime Value of a Client (LVC)

Do you notice two things we talk about that are not on the list? Clients and revenue.

Isn't that interesting? That's because clients and revenue are lagging indicators. They are the result of your leading indicators. You cannot impact clients and revenue. You can only change what creates them.

Clients are the product of leads and conversions. You can improve the quality or quantity of your leads and the conversion rate through skill development, messaging, and process. The result of these changes is a change in clients. Let's define these a little further.

Leads

A *lead* in business, also called a sales lead, is a consumer interested in what your company offers. This varies from business to business, but it always "leads" you to a sale. In my world, a lead is a potential client who has signified in some way that they are interested. That interest could come up to me at a networking meeting, a website visit, a free gift opt-in, a phone call, or an email.

To attract more leads, you have two main options: ramp up your marketing efforts or refine your marketing message. We will talk about leads first and conversions next.

As we start talking about leads, let's first define marketing and sales. There are so many ways words are used in business, and they often vary from person to person. For today, we will use these definitions:

Marketing: The process of generating a lead.

Sales: The process of *converting* that lead into a client and servicing them to the fullest potential.

Sales and marketing go together like peanut butter and jelly on a sandwich. The "peanut butter" is the sales, and the "jelly" is the marketing. You put them "on the bread" of what your business does to solve a problem for others.

Have you ever tried to pull apart a peanut butter and jelly sandwich? You get tendrils of jelly stretching between the two slices of bread. You get chunks of peanut butter lodged in the jelly. It can be messy. That is the way I see sales and marketing in a business. They profoundly influence each other.

Good marketing starts the sales conversation from the first interaction. It is not about brand awareness. It is about your ability to communicate the brand proposition you refined in an earlier chapter. It is about claiming a niche, knowing the problem you solve, why that's important to your niche (not why it is important to you), and what the benefits and change look like to your client. This is the WIIFM factor ("What's In It For Me"). Marketing gets people's interest and promotes action.

You must adjust your sales and marketing components if you have trouble attracting new clients. Many business owners looking to grow their client base, only count how many clients are coming through the door. Instead, they should take a step back and track their leads.

Tracking Leads

Most business owners accept tracking numbers. I hear the occasional complaint that it is boring or that someone doesn't like math, so they don't want to do it. There is nothing sexy about tracking, and there won't be any if you look at tracking like it is work.

Instead, imagine tracking as your ability to generate profits.

How do you track leads?

You can track the leads, or potentially interested clients, any way you want. You can have a program dedicated to tracking it, use a spreadsheet, and make notes on your phone. For that matter, you can simply put hashtags on the back of an envelope in your purse. It really does not matter how—as long as you do.

Mark how many leads you needed before you made a sale. Track this number every time to see if your pattern stays the same.

I'll eventually want you to track which of your marketing efforts are generating the lead, but let's start by benchmarking your leads. Future enhancements can automate the process of tracking them.

Conversions

Conversion refers to the act of turning a lead into a paying customer, subscriber, or client. Boosting your conversion rate is the second way to create more clients.

You can boost the conversion rate by improving your marketing message, sales process, sales communication, sales team, and/or sales skills.

A great example of conversions in action

Think back to when you were a kid around an ice cream truck. I grew up in the sweltering, humid heat of Houston. Summers can be brutal. You could hear the ice cream truck driving closer to you when it was still streets away. As kids, if we were outside—we would all stop what we were doing and head to the house to find some money. We NEEDED ice cream! If we weren't back on the street before the truck came down the street, we would miss out or have to race to the next street. With luck, once we found our money, we ran back to the street, found some shade, and waited. When the ice cream truck stopped, a line of kids was waiting with money in hand, ready to buy just about anything.

What do you think the ice cream truck's conversion rate was? It was probably pretty high because the business model was set on volume at an accessible price. It was an easy buy because you could almost always find the fifty cents or a dollar it took to buy one. There wasn't much of a purchase decision involved.

Now, people easily pay $10-12 for the experience of picking their ice cream and toppings and having someone mix it together for them, as they pay for it by weight. What do you think their conversion is? It's high for people who walk through the door.

Both businesses face the challenge of getting people to the door. Once they are at the door, they are easy to convert. These two businesses, with different business models in the same industry, have high conversion rates.

What is a good conversion rate?

You will need to track your numbers to discover a good conversion rate for your business. It's only that *good* is subjective. Your conversion is only good or bad in the context of your business, model and environment. Our goal is for the conversion rate to be maximally effective for the price.

In my first business, my conversion rate was 80 percent. I was proud of that number. Now, I recognize that I was not where I needed to be for the business model I wanted to pursue. Current-Me would tell Past-Me to increase my pricing based on the conversion rate and the rest of the business's KPIs.

Past clients have had conversion rates ranging between 20 percent to 40 percent, depending on the service offering, which is a great number for them.

As a rule of thumb, the lower your price, the higher your conversion. The higher your price, the lower your conversion. This represents an inverse relationship between price and conversion.

When the conversion is high, especially for a service-based business, it is more than likely a business that can look at multiple revenue streams, entertain bringing in service levels, or just flat-out raise your prices.

If my conversion rate is high, should I always raise my prices?

We aren't big fans of raising prices just to raise prices. It needs to be strategic, and all numbers need to be evaluated before considering a rate change. While conversion rate is a key indicator, it is important to consider other factors completely.

For instance, will a higher price align with the overall market and competitive landscape? In addition, think about the timing of the price increase. Is your industry facing any economic downturns or upturns?

Changing rates based on one metric alone would be like taking medicine at the doctor's office without considering the other indicators of what might be going on.

Calculating Your Conversion Rate

The conversion rate is a metric with a little math behind it. To determine your conversion rate, assess your leads for a given time frame (per month, per quarter, per year). You can take the number of new clients for that same time and perform the following math:

Clients ÷ Leads = Conversion Rate

We used this example earlier. For the sake of working through the KPIs, let's revisit. Our example calculates your conversion rate:

10 Clients ÷ 35 Leads = 28.6% Conversion

Leads and conversions, when combined, tell us about our clients. If your growth plan is about generating more clients, these KPIs will be helpful. However, two other numbers indicate if you are leaving money on the table or if your business could run more efficiently. If that is the case, improving these KPIs is easier and more cost-effective than getting more clients. These two numbers are the average sales per client and the average number of purchases per client. These numbers look at the same information sales as they relate to client, but they consider how much a client purchases in dollars and how frequently they purchase.

Average Sales Per Client

Have you ever wondered how much revenue each of your customers brings in? Tracking your Average Sales Per Client helps you see exactly that, allowing you to identify your most valuable clients. It also shows how effective your sales strategies are and highlights opportunities for growth. By focusing on this metric, you can make smarter decisions to boost your revenue, improve customer targeting, and enhance your overall business strategy.

Your average sale per client is simple math. If you took your total sales (income or revenue) and divided that number by the number of clients, you would get to your average sale.

Let's say your total sales were $323,034 across 10 clients. Then, your calculation would look like this:

$323,034 ÷ 10 clients = $32,303.40/client

This is important to watch as a KPI, as it tells you a few things:

If the trend of your average sale increases, it speaks well to your ability to sell and serve your client—it can show that the business is maturing and progressing.

If the trend declines, it could signal a *review* of your marketing and sales messages. Are you attracting the right client?

Whatever way this metric trends, asking critical questions to understand the trend will help you make better decisions and determine the best strategic path forward.

For instance, the decision to strategically increase your average sales per client has the benefit of bringing ease into your business. It is more favorable as the increase in sales per client reduces the need for as many clients to produce the same revenue.

This impact directly improves your quality of life, enabling you to work less to produce the same result. As pricing is a tactic that can be used to improve this indicator, an upward trend in average sales could also lead to improved profitability.

An Example From One of Our Clients

We reviewed the average sale for a client and noticed an interesting trend. Sales increased steadily over the first two years, then suddenly dropped in the third year and stayed low in the fourth year. The business owner was puzzled. Revenue was flat, everyone was busy, and profitability was declining because it seemed to take more resources to handle the work.

We found the answer when we dug deeper and examined the types of sales by product or service. In 2020, the team had adapted to their clients' shifting needs. Clients moved away from big projects with big budgets and opted for smaller commitments since they were converting well. The team stuck with what was working.

However, as the economy recovered, they never adjusted their strategy back. This focus on smaller commitments concentrated on the least profitable work, impacting overall profitability.

We worked with them to market toward the more impactful work and got the business back on track.

Average Number of Purchases per Client

The metric that shows the average quantity of client purchases helps businesses understand how often their customers purchase over a given period.

It indicates if there are repeat purchases or if the client only purchases once from you in a year. This metric gives you insight into your customers' buying behavior, indicating loyalty and, potentially, how satisfied your clients are with your product or services.

This metric is also important, as improving it can have an exponential impact on your business's growth and health.

To determine the metric, divide the number or quantity of invoices or sales by the number of clients. You will get the average times a client purchases.

$$\textit{\# of Sales} \div \textit{\# of Clients} = \textit{Average Purchases Per Client}$$

For the 10 clients above, if there were 15 sales, then the average times purchased would be the following:

$$\textit{15 Sales} \div \textit{10 Clients} = \textit{1.5 (Average Purchases per Client)}$$

How Do I Define a Purchase?

Total Sales, Income, and Revenue are the sum of all purchases. But, the definition of a purchase can be a bit tricky because it is a subjective choice. There's no right or wrong way. It only matters that you choose one way and stay consistent.

Here are a couple of decisions you could make. Maybe you have a project (possibly one sale) with multiple invoices (possibly multiple sales). Which one do you choose? Is it one sale or multiple sales? In this case, I'm a proponent of "by the project" since each separate invoice in the sale cannot stand independently. So, I would count it as one.

In another scenario, perhaps you have clients who are on a subscription for a service and pay every month. Is that one sale or 12 for the year? In this case, I'm a proponent of 12 because the purchase decision is made every month. Don't overthink this (even though it is easy to do)—just define how you look at it and maintain that view.

The Importance of This Metric

This metric is important because it amplifies how easy or difficult it feels to grow your business. Would you like to know what makes a business difficult? *No repeat purchases during the year.* That challenges real estate agents, photographers, construction companies, designers, etc. If you are a "one-and-done" type of transaction, your marketing and sales engine must be top-notch.

Here is the power of this metric in real life. The business we were reviewing was averaging 1.2 purchases per client. Yet, their model and value proposition were built on relationships and serving clients who would need their services regularly. To understand the metric, we dug into the marketing and sales of the business. We identified that the business owner unconsciously focused on clients who needed one instance of their service rather than a client who needed two or more instances. This little shift would double the business in nine months. The business could boast multiple client relationships with four or more repeat client purchases three years later.

As an advanced move, you could apply this metric back to average sales to get average sales per purchase. The math would look like this:

Total Sales (\$) ÷ # of Purchases = Average Sales Per Purchase

The result would be:

\$323,034 ÷ 15 Purchases = \$21,535.60

An Easy Way to Double Your Business

An easy way to double your business is to double the average number of times purchased. Let's consider product businesses and service businesses as two different scenarios.

Product-based businesses can see a quicker increase in purchases, as they tend to be more consumable products. However, higher-end products that are not consumable and service businesses tend to see a more gradual improvement. For instance, improving from 1.2 to 1.3 purchases is more likely. However, some strategies can invite the client to purchase a second time in a year. Let's look at one of my favorites.

Understanding the Problem-Solution, Problem-Solution Strategy

Reflecting back on the value proposition, this strategy enables you to outline a client journey across products or services based on their problems.

Start by recognizing the first problem that you solve for clients. Once you understand that, ask yourself, "If I solve my client's problem, what will be the next problem they have?" Then, find a way to solve that one. Keep going until you run out of options.

You will be able to continue your client relationship by doing this exercise. You will have a business that feels easy, and the exercise reduces your dependency on the next new client. It will help you find efficiencies that come with a long-term, mutually beneficial relationship with your client.

If you suffer from the "one-and-done" situation, and this strategy won't work because you are too good at what you do, then there is one more option. This may be the time to look at your service delivery and decide if you could break it apart into stages to go deeper into each stage and then get repeat purchases with each subsequent stage.

Gross and Net Profit Margins

As we discussed in our pricing chapter, profit doesn't just happen. It is planned for and crafted. Understanding your gross and net profit margins is essential to this planning.

Gross Profit is the profit your company makes after deducting the costs directly associated with producing and selling its products or services.

Net profit is your company's total earnings after all expenses, including operating costs, taxes, and interest, have been deducted from total revenue.

Margin represents the percentage of either gross profit or net profit relative to revenue. These are often represented in dollars ($) or referred to as Gross and Net Income.

Profit margins are influenced by several factors, including your business model, pricing structure (how much you sell for versus how much it costs to create), business size, and whether you offer products, services, or a combination of both.

In pure service businesses, you can have excellent, healthy profitability. If you have a hybrid, your revenue is probably larger, but depending on the cost of goods and the supply chain, you could see a lower profit percentage. If it is a product-based business, you could see even higher revenues and possibly an even lower profit margin. As with our other KPIs, the metric is relative to many factors. If a business demonstrated a 20 percent net profit margin, it would be impossible to determine whether that margin was good, as the information is almost irrelevant without context.

What You Should Know

Economies of Scale: As your business grows, you can use economies of scale to improve profitability. This means leveraging your purchasing power and manufacturing capacity to reduce costs.

Gross Profit Margin (GPM): A financial metric that shows the percentage of revenue that exceeds the cost of goods sold (COGS). It measures how efficiently a company is producing and selling its products or services.

Net Profit Margin (NPM): A financial metric that indicates the percentage of revenue that remains as profit after all expenses have been deducted. This is the bottom line of your profitability. It measures the overall profitability after all operational expenses are deducted from your gross profit.

Yet, for all the variability, there are hard truths about profitability. For instance, if your Gross Profit Margin (GPM) is less than 40 percent, it's typically exceedingly challenging to get a positive Net Profit. Even when your GPM is 40–60 percent, it is still pretty challenging. Our goal for all our businesses is a minimal 60 percent for product and hybrid business models. Service businesses typically operate at 95 percent or higher.

There are two ways to look at gross and net profit in dollars and percentages. Let's tackle Gross Profit and Margin first.

Gross Profit: Above the line

If you've ever heard the phrase "above the line," this refers to Gross Profit from your Profit & Loss Statement. Your statement may look a little like this simplified version:

Profit and Loss Statement

Income
    Income-Sales of Product Income
    Refunds Given
    Sales of Product Income
    Services
Total Income
Cost of Goods Sold
    Material Purchases-COGS
    Salaries & Wages-COGS
    Shipping, Freight & Delivery - COGS
    Supplies - COGS
Total Cost of Goods Sold
GROSS PROFIT

In the above example, income or sales are followed by the Cost of Goods Sold (COGS) and Gross Profit. (If you have a service-based business and do not hire outside labor, you may not have COGS.) The math looks like this:

Total Income - Total COGS = Gross Profits

For the period, let's say you produced $150,000 in income and your COGS $65,000. The resulting math would be:

$150,000 - $65,000 = $85,000

For this period, the business produced $85,000 in Gross Profit. *Gross Profit Margin* is the relationship of your Gross Profit to your Total Income. The resulting math is this:

$$\textbf{\textit{Gross Profit ÷ Total income = Gross Profit Margin}}$$

With our numbers, it looks like this:

$$\textbf{\textit{\$85,000 ÷ \$150,000 = 56.6\%}}$$

Net Profit: The Bottom Line

After Gross Profit on your P&L, everything below it is considered "below the line." If you hear that phrase, it generally refers to everything in your expenses. This area is also referred to as Operational Expenses or OPEX. These expenses are necessary for the operation of the business and include fixed costs—rent and utilities—and variable costs—training, professional services, etc. At the bottom of your statement, you'll find Net Income. Net Income is considered "the bottom line."

Again, if we simplify the P&L to hide detail, here is the structure:

Profit and Loss Statement

Total Income
Total Cost of Goods Sold
GROSS PROFIT
Total Expenses
NET INCOME

The math to derive Net Income is the following:

$$\textbf{\textit{Gross Profit - Total Expenses = Net Income}}$$

From our working numbers, let's assume that Total Expenses for the period were $45,000. We bring forth the $65,000 in Gross Profit for this next step:

$$\$65,0000 - \$45,000 = \$20,000$$

This business achieved \$20,000 in Net Income or Profit for this period. To find the Net Profit Margin, our formula looks like this:

$$\textbf{\textit{Net Income} ÷ \textit{Total Income} = \textit{Net Profit Margin}}$$

or, in our example:

$$\$20,000 ÷ \$150,000 = 13\%$$

The ratios of Gross Profit Margin (GPM) and Net Profit Margin (NPM) are the ratios we, as a team of strategists looking at your business from an outside perspective, run first. They are reliable indicators of business health and point where to go first. These lagging indicators can be used as leading indicators if you track your profitability per job and set baseline KPIs for all your projects. Depending on your stage of business growth, your breakeven point is when you cover your expenses. When you exceed the breakeven point, then you can be profitable.

Takeaways for Your Business

Track Your Margins: Gross and net profit margins are reliable indicators of business health. They help you understand where your money is going and where you might need to make adjustments.

Set Baseline KPIs: Use these margins as Key Performance Indicators (KPIs) to track your profitability per job or project.
Breakeven Point: Knowing your breakeven point—the point at which you cover all expenses—is crucial. Beyond this point, your business starts to become profitable.

By regularly monitoring and understanding these financial metrics, you can make informed decisions that drive sustainable growth and profitability in your business.

Cost of Acquisition (COA)

The Cost of Acquisition (COA) refers to the total expense incurred by a company to acquire a new customer, including all marketing and sales-related costs.

To calculate it, you will divide the marketing dollars you have spent (or monetize your time) by the number of clients generated.

$$\textit{Marketing \$} \div \textit{Clients Generated} = \textit{COA}$$

If your company spent \$13,256 in marketing and generated 12 clients, then the math would be:

$$\$13,\!256 \div 10 \text{ clients} = \$1,\!325.60$$

Marketers like this number because it helps them determine if the money spent on advertising is paying off—that's what they call *Return on Investment*, or ROI. They'll often show this number to highlight how effective their marketing strategies are for a business.

Interestingly, many business owners don't know this number or fully grasp its importance. Understanding it can help you decide where to invest your marketing dollars wisely so you're spending money and making more in return.

Why Most Business Owners Don't Understand Their COA

The simplest reason is that business owners aren't taught to monitor their marketing this way. However, your COA is a way to measure the effectiveness of your marketing. When you rely entirely on intuition or how you feel about marketing, you could stop a successful effort or continue one that doesn't meet its goals.

Our approach is that everything you invest in for marketing should be expected to generate leads. Often, you can tell which leads and clients come from which marketing efforts. With this information, you can look at the COA across the organization and individually for each marketing effort.

These efforts should be evaluated quarterly and annually to refine your marketing plan and ensure that the money you invest gives something back.

Should I Try to Raise or Lower My COA?

Like Conversion Rate and Profit, the Cost of Acquisition is a relative number. Your goal is not to raise or lower it; your goal is to maximize its effectiveness and likelihood of conversion.

If you knew you could spend $1,325 and generate an average sale of $32,303.40, would you? Probably every day of the week, it's a 24.38 return on your investment. That means every $1 invested generated $24.38 in revenue.

In my first business, the acquisition cost was $500 and generated $65,000 in revenue. However, a high-volume realtor friend thought the COA was incredibly high. For him, his COA was $165 and yielded $7,500. Which is better?

No matter the cost, the goal is to ensure that this investment is profitable, which is where Return on Investment (ROI) comes into play. For my first business, the ROI (Sales ÷ COA) was a multiplier of 130. Our realtor friend saw a multiplier of 45. Our fictional business for this chapter sees a multiplier of 24. All of these are excellent baselines.

At the bare minimum, we want you to see a multiplier of five for the return. For instance, if you spend $100 on marketing to acquire a new client, you should aim for this expense to generate significantly more revenue. At a minimum, you'd want to see $500 in revenue from this expenditure, which gives you a 5x return on your initial investment.

From what we see across all industries and businesses, the return should be much more significant, more like a 10x return, meaning that your $100 investment should ideally generate $1,000 in revenue. This higher multiplier covers your initial cost and substantially increases your profit, making your marketing efforts highly effective and justifiable.

When used in combination with our next figure, you can have a powerhouse revenue-producing machine.

Lifetime Value of a Client (LVC)

The Lifetime Value of a Client represents the total revenue a business can expect from a single customer throughout their entire relationship with the company.

How long do your clients stay with you? Again, if you are a "one-and-done" type of business, maybe not long. If the work takes time to produce, but the client returns once a year for every year, that's reliable.

Even businesses that go five to seven years between purchases need to think about staying connected with their clients during these intervals. It's crucial to keep engaging with these customers through targeted marketing to ensure your business remains at the top of their minds. If you've ever had a past client tell you they forgot you could handle something for them, this is your problem.

By understanding how long customers typically stick with you, you can tailor your communication strategies effectively. Ongoing engagement helps ensure that when they are ready to make another purchase, your business is the first one they think of, thus maximizing the lifetime value they offer your company over the years.

With that information—here's the math:

$$\textit{Average Sale} \times \textit{Avg \# Purchases} \times \textit{\# of years} =$$
$$\textit{Lifetime Value of a Client (LVC)}$$

Let's break down how you can determine how much a customer is worth to your business over the time they stay with you. Here's a simple way to do the math:

1. *Average Sale:* How much money you typically make from one sale to a customer.
2. *Average Number of Purchases:* How many times a customer buys from you in a year.
3. *Number of Years:* How many years has the customer returned to buy from you?
4. *Multiply these three things* to give you the LVC.

So, if your company had $32,303.40 for the average sale with an average number of 1.5 purchases in a year across five years, the lifetime value of a client would be:

$$\$32,303.40 \times 1.5 \text{ purchases} \times 5 \text{ years} = \$242,275.50$$

The LVC is a super helpful number because it tells you how much you can afford to spend on attracting and keeping each customer and still making a profit. It also emphasizes the importance of maintaining a client relationship between purchases.

While this is typically a scaling move, we need to discuss this scenario in the context of the KPI, as this strategy can change the course of your business. The strength of maximizing your LVC can improve almost every other KPI. While most KPIs discussed are often reviewed in the context of a year, this KPI is about creating long-term sustainability in your business. Let's look at a case study to understand the potential better.

Case Study: Looking at a Business with Long Repeat Cycles

In another client study, we had a business with extensive initial projects. They did a great job, and the project's impact on the business's financials represented the performance. Their clients raved over the experience, leaving five-star reviews. However, because each project is intense, once a project is complete, their attention turns to the next project that needs to be delivered to completion. Years could pass, and they would suddenly see the client complete their next project with a new firm. What happened to the five-star, happy client? Simple, the firm, in trying to get the next project done, did not stay top of mind with the client.

When we devised a strategy to maintain touch, seize repeat sales, and contribute to revenue more regularly, we could implement a multi-layered approach. This approach not only ensured a steady stream of revenue but also fostered a stronger relationship with the client, increasing the likelihood of repeat business.

Based on that purchase cycle, we mapped a sales timeline, using the same approach as Problem-Solution from the average purchase KPI.

Putting Together COA and LVC

Let's discuss how you can invest smartly in your marketing by understanding two key numbers: the COA and the LVC.

Imagine you're thinking about spending $15,000 on a marketing campaign. Here's how you figure out if that's a wise move:

First, you must know that attracting each new client costs you about $1,325 (COA). Over time, each client brings about $242,275.50 (LVC) to your business. Let's run the math.

$$\textbf{\textit{Marketing Investment} ÷ \textit{COA}}$$
$$\textbf{\textit{= Anticipated \# of Clients Generated}}$$
$$\textbf{\textit{\$15,000 ÷ \$1,325 = 11.32 Clients}}$$

If you put down $15,000, theoretically, you should get about 11 new clients (rounded down).

Now, consider your conversion rate; from the beginning of the chapter, we found that it is 28.6 percent.

$$\textbf{\textit{Anticipated \# of Clients ÷ Conversion}}$$
$$\textbf{\textit{= Anticipated \# of Leads Generated}}$$
$$\textbf{\textit{11 clients ÷ .28 conversion rate = 39.286 Leads}}$$

To get those 11 new clients, you need to reach about 39 leads because only a portion of them will convert to clients. The question we ask here is, how likely is that to happen in the same calendar year? What does your intuition and knowledge of your sales cycle tell you to do?

That's how you use the COA and LVC to make real-world decisions.

No marketing effort comes with guarantees, but understanding your COA and LVC helps you make smarter, safer bets with your marketing dollars. Every business needs investment in marketing. With the knowledge of how to manage through your KPIs, you can marry intuition and data. You'll also shift your expectation of your marketing efforts. If every marketing dollar has a job to bring revenue and clients to your door, which of your current efforts would stay? Which needs improving, or just dropped altogether?

The Power of the Seven Essential Metrics

These essential metrics act as powerful tools to forecast and drive your business's future growth. To recap, the seven metrics are:

1. Leads
2. Conversion Rate

   —Clients—

3. Average Sale Per Client
4. Average # of Purchases

   —Revenue—
   —Gross Profit—

5. Net Profitability
6. Lifetime Value of a Client
7. Cost of Client Acquisition

Clients, Revenue, and Gross Profit are included because they are important, but they are not part of the seven metrics as they are lagging indicators and are the result of the seven metrics that can be changed.

Think of each metric as an ingredient that we mix and experiment with. As we tweak each metric slightly, like adjusting ingredients in a recipe, we start to see how these small changes can have a compound effect. Each adjustment might seem minor, but together, they can lead to significant growth, transforming your business's overall picture and performance.

How Can We Apply the Power of KPIs?

Let's go back to our marketing example and begin to see the compound effect we can create with simple tweaks in the business. You already know for your $15,000 marketing investment:

- It costs $1,325 to acquire each new client.
- Each client, on average, brings $242,275 to your business over their lifetime.

- If you spend $15,000 and it costs $1,325 to get a client, you could bring in 11 new clients.

But what if you improve your conversion rates or increase the average purchase amount? Let's say you increase your conversion to 40 percent; instead of 39 leads, you only need 28.

What if you also included a 10 percent price increase? LVC would increase from $242,275 for 11 clients to $266,502. Both scenarios increase revenue and decrease COA. Do both, and you begin to see exponential results.

The Magic in Looking at These Seven Metrics

Once we have a business's baseline to work with, we look at growth across each metric at the rate of 10 percent to 50 percent and then that growth's cumulative impact across all seven numbers.

As we illustrated with our marketing COA, you can achieve exponential growth with minor changes. If you made small changes and increased each of your first four metrics by 10 percent, the result for your overall business growth could be around 46 percent. That's significant and changes how your business operates.

Working with our client's vision and goals, we evaluate the intentional growth at each major metric and determine our growth expectations.

After we've set the intention for our growth, we can formulate the strategies and priorities to make the growth possible.

Identifying When It's Not Time to Grow

Looking at your growth forecast can show a tremendous opportunity for the future and tell you when there are serious problems. By making strategic models, you can work on fixing the issues before turning your intention to growth.

Real-World Example

When a business went through our audit process, we were determining what and where the opportunity for their growth journey existed, and a red flag popped up. This warning strongly said that it was not time to grow.

At six months old, this was our client's second business, and it was doing well, delivering a highly successful and impactful service.

The owners came to us with the request to help them find a way to get more clients. Before we even started talking about potential strategies to do that, I wanted to look at their seven KPIs. I've listed them out for you:

1.	Leads	22
2.	Conversion Rate	73%
	—Clients—	16
3.	Average Sale Per Client	$1,419.38
4.	Average # of Purchases	1.125
	—Gross Profit—	$22,710.00
5.	Net Profit	-65%
6.	Lifetime Value of a Client	$1,419.38
7.	Cost of Client Acquisition	$1,250.00

What jumps out when you look at these numbers?

The Problem

Hopefully, the net profit would be one of the biggest indicators since it is negative. However, this isn't crazy, as this was still a young company. It's the last two figures that worry me.

- LVC was $1,419
- COA was $1,250

I am not worried about the amount of money that is spent on gaining the client. It was a little high for what they do, but not crazy. I was concerned about the ratio.

For every $1,250 spent on marketing, they made $1,419, a difference of $169.

That only left $169 to cover operational expenses, feed into marketing, pay for salaries, and all the little things in a business. Essentially, it is safe to assume that they were losing money on every client, and the net profit margin confirms this.

If we were to implement strategies to double their clients, what do you think would happen to their business?

It would go broke, and more clients would destroy the business. I began to share that with them first: "You are not ready to grow, and here's why…"

The Fix

The fix was easy to see. Let's see if you can see it too. The first hint came with the average purchases. It was 1.125, so virtually a one. This is a hint of the "one-and-done" problem.

The second hint comes with their conversion rate, a whopping 73 percent! In asking a few questions, I discovered how well this company solves their ideal client's problems. They solve it so well that their clients don't need to buy from my clients ever again.

Then we talked about sales conversion, and almost everyone said yes. Wouldn't you say yes to a solution that was working for 100 percent of the people and was bargain basement pricing?

People are smart. When they see a good deal, they jump all over it.

Opportunities

What I saw were two opportunities:

1. Increase the price because the conversions demonstrated price elasticity. With the proper value positioning, they could easily double their pricing.
2. They were either over-delivering (and not charging enough), solving problems too quickly (leading to clients undervaluing their services), or missing additional revenue opportunities by not identifying the next problem they could solve for their clients.

Working with that information, here is the plan we devised for the next six months:

- Boost the leads by two each month—which is necessary to offset the change we will create in the conversion rate.
- Raise the prices and expect the conversion rate to drop (*which almost always happens*).
- Based on the solution's value, increase the average sale (*which still represented savings for the client*).
- Break apart the service offering into a two-part series. This allows the clients to work deeper, experience lasting transformation, and encourage them to purchase again.

The impact of a few changes like these is huge on a business. They create a more cash-stable business ready to grow, and the cash generated can be used to pay for more marketing, teams, systems, and the like.

Personalized Strategies for Growth to Maximum Impact

It's important to recognize that identifying growth opportunities involves more than exploring new markets or adding to your product line. It requires a proactive and strategic mindset. You must observe, adapt, and take decisive action, even when uncertain. You set your business up not just to survive but to thrive by tracking the right metrics and responding effectively to their insights.

Choosing the right strategies for your business is a customized process. Success means understanding your unique business model, vision, and customer base. With this understanding, we can align these elements with your KPIs to develop tailored recommendations. This book gives you the foundational knowledge and process, but the specific strategies that align with your goals need a personalized approach.

Start by running your KPIs for the last three years of your business. What story do they tell? Three years is enough to spot trends and use them to create a more profitable future. Monitoring your KPIs helps you understand your business's strengths and vulnerabilities. Remember, each KPI has its own monthly, quarterly, or annual review schedule. Working them into a regular process and taking time to understand them allows you to be flexible in your strategic decisions, enabling you to pivot or adjust your strategies as needed.

KPIs also help you spot potential risks or issues early. Recognizing these risks before they escalate, you can adapt proactively, mitigating threats to your business. This proactive approach is a key component of resilience, allowing you to address challenges before they become critical problems.

This continuous monitoring and adjustment helps your business to stay stable and quickly recover from disruptions. Each challenge you encounter, and every data point you evaluate, offers valuable insights to inform your strategic decisions, shifting your approach from merely reactive to robustly proactive.

In our next chapter, we shift our focus from finding opportunities to fortifying your business against inevitable challenges. The approach allows businesses to withstand crises and emerge stronger from them. It operates as a defense mechanism and a dynamic tool for sustainable success.

Chapter 12

YOUR GROWTH MINDSET
Resilience Reimagined
for Business Success

"But little mouse, you're not alone,
In finding that foresight can be in vain:
The best-laid plans of mice and men
Often go wrong,"
—"To A Mouse,"
poem by Robert Burns, 1785

Even the best-laid plans can go awry. If you've ever found your carefully crafted plans derailed unexpectedly, take comfort—you're not alone. When it comes to managing growth, this poem reminds us that things can unexpectedly change.

In business, as in life, unexpected challenges and disruptions are inevitable. The question is not *if* they will happen but *when*. This may seem to conflict with the work of the last chapter. On the contrary, this concept only reinforces that a strategic planning framework is necessary to reduce the risk of being caught off guard.

This chapter explores what happens when you implement strategies and have the inevitable happen. In these moments, it is about surviving these moments and thriving through them. We will explore how to keep a growth mindset to forge ahead and make great decisions even when business doesn't happen as you thought it would.

Resilience is the Key

Resilience is the ability to recover swiftly from setbacks and adapt effectively, even in adversity, stress, or unforeseen changes. In business, resilience involves maintaining functionality and rapidly returning to a stable state after experiencing a disruption. It allows a business to withstand crises and emerge stronger from them.

As a business owner, you face unique challenges that make resilience essential. With limited resources, your business is often more vulnerable to market fluctuations, shifts in customer demand, or supply chain disruptions. The financial and emotional investment you pour into your venture means any setbacks can impact your business operations and personal life.

Resilience is a dynamic tool for sustainable success. It operates as a defense mechanism and an adaptive strength that allows businesses to navigate uncertainties and ensure long-term sustainability and success.

What do you do when business isn't going your way?

Instead of panicking or freezing, a resilient business adapts and grows stronger. At its core, resilience is your ability to recover swiftly from setbacks and adapt effectively even with adversity, stress, or unforeseen changes. In both personal and professional contexts, resilience involves maintaining functionality and rapidly returning to a stable state after experiencing a disruption.

For individuals, resilience means bouncing back from setbacks with a renewed sense of strength and resolve. It often involves psychological resilience when one finds personal growth during difficult times. This personal resilience is crucial for emotional and mental health, helping individuals cope with stress, overcome challenges, and move forward more robustly.

In a business context, resilience refers to an organization's ability to withstand crises and bounce back from hardships, such as economic recessions, supply chain disruptions, or sudden losses of critical resources. It encompasses restoring business operations and services to normal, learning, and growing from the experience as you improve future responsiveness and adaptability.

Resilient businesses plan for potential difficulties, adapting their operations and strategies to mitigate the impacts of shocks and stresses. They also cultivate a culture of resilience by promoting flexibility, proactive problem-solving, and continuous improvement among their workforce. It makes the organization better equipped to navigate uncertainties and ensures long-term sustainability and success.

You'll face plenty of setbacks—each one might feel harder than the last and push you close to giving up. But the kind of resilience we talk about here isn't just about getting back on your feet; it's about coming back stronger, with more energy and clearer vision each time.

Even when you're unsure where to find the strength to continue, there's always hope. There's always a way to make a comeback, especially if you think of resilience as something you practice regularly, like a skill that improves the more you work on it.

The practice begins with mindfulness that anchors you in the present moment, enabling clear, focused decision-making in the chaos. You can recognize the moment for what it is as you experience the emotions of disappointment, frustration, and aggravation. To feel is to be human.

It is only an issue when you stay in the emotion and do not allow it to pass over you. When this happens, you get stuck in a fixed mindset. Know that if you get here—you're not alone. You are being called to transform into a better leader.

Leadership Transformation: A Look into My Journey

Reflecting on my journey, there are distinct moments—three or four pivotal times—when I had to evolve significantly as both a leader and a person to meet my business goals.

The first was when I chose to find a different path for my business after the recession. Losing 50 percent of my first business in a blindsided moment was crushing. It would take me three years to see the need for transformation. The second was when I chose to find a different business for my soul, and I realized that what I had built did not serve my personal goals. Even though it was my decision, I expected a subtle transformation and was greeted instead with an opportunity for the transformation to be more extensive. The third was when I became "more" to create a greater impact and leave a legacy of building better businesses. I'll admit this one was a little easier, maybe because I had made the changes before. But it was still hard. I was simply more accustomed to the process. Can you pinpoint these transformational moments and why they were necessary for you?

On paper, these transformations sound simple. But when I consider them, I realize that each change was motivated by a different factor. The first change was motivated by fear. The second change was motivated by the desire for a better quality of life. The third change was motivated by the desire to have more impact.

Before I accepted the challenge of transforming how I showed up in the world, I went through anger and resentment. Changing who you are and how you show up forces you to deal with your baggage, which is not always fun. Yet, we all know that change is our only constant. We must evolve and adapt to this ever-changing world.

This process of evolution is similar to what I imagine a caterpillar must go through to transform into a butterfly. Encasing itself into a cocoon, the caterpillar effectively dissolves into goo to reform into the structure of the butterfly. I can only imagine the pain and uncertainty at that moment, not to mention the energy that goes into the re-creation process. This process then culminates when the butterfly must free itself from the cocoon, the ultimate expression of a final push through a self-imposed barrier. It's a wonder that they are compelled to transform. In truth, they do it because they do not have a choice.

There are many different ways to look at up-leveling your business. Today, we will look at it from the perspective of adopting a different operating mode when change is the last thing you want.

You and I have established in the journey of this book that change is constant and that growth happens just past our comfort level. It's human to want things to stay the same as they always have been. That is comfort and routine.

Because changes consistently occur, your success is tied to your ability to harness change to benefit yourself, your team, and your business. This conflicts with the human desire for comfort and routine.

So, what do you do when change happens? Do you adjust and move on? Do you fight it or freeze up? All too commonly, when someone first starts their business, they would adjust and move on. But, after a while, they get tired and burned out. When change happens at that point, they fight it, ignore it, or they just freeze up. If that is you, let's look at the hard costs of flight or freeze.

Understanding Fixed and Growth Mindsets

Carol Dweck, a psychologist and author of *Mindset: The New Psychology of Success*, first introduced the concept of fixed and growth mindsets. In her work, she studied young students to determine the qualities that determined success. She observed that some people meet adversity and fall apart, while others meet the challenge and persevere. She named these two approaches as having a "fixed" and a "growth" mindset.

The response of flight/freeze activates and feeds a *fixed mindset*. This is where you believe you are "good" or "bad" at things and will always be so. It is predicated on believing that you are what you are and can become no more—no matter what you do. You're effectively locked in a self-imposed cocoon.

Dweck found that continually operating from a fixed mindset led to fewer opportunities and declining success. In essence, it created a downward spiral. Staying locked in a fixed mindset stifles your ability to grow, scale, and take new chances.

Conversely, operating in a *growth mindset* sets your success into an upward spiral where incremental growth and success become more accessible and easier. A growth mindset believes in the ability to become more than you are today, whether through knowledge, experience, or effort.

People with a growth mindset demonstrate resilience by picking themselves up, dusting off their scraped knees, and trying again.

Do You Have a Fixed Mindset or a Growth Mindset?

Is your mindset fixed or geared toward growth? While it's tempting to think of this as a black-and-white issue, the reality is much more complex.

Working with our business owners over the years, it has become clear that your mindset shifts with the topic and confidence around it.

For instance, you could exhibit a fixed mindset about sales, thinking they have to stay exactly as they are, and a growth mindset about doing the work of the business, where you are open to change. In one area, you feel at a loss. In another, you feel like an expert.

The key to success is to acknowledge where you may be operating in a fixed mindset, not willing to consider your options, and where you are operating in a growth mindset, making changes as needed.

You must evaluate what staying in a fixed mindset costs you. You may need to check yourself to see if it creates stagnation, an inability to adapt, or missed opportunities.

Your role as the business leader is to manage with the ideals of growth, resilience, integrity, and tenacity. That requires operating from a growth mindset as your default operating system.

Realizing Resilience:
The Real Payoff to Adopting a Growth Mindset

The biggest payoff to adopting a growth mindset is that you stay in the game. You use *persistence* (continuing with something even though it is difficult) and turn that into *tenacity* (determination and not giving up easily) to stay committed to the goal.

The belief that anything is possible if you set your mind to it allows you to create beautiful results. Growing a business successfully requires you to conduct experiments along the way. These experiments prove or disprove your assumptions. That means some will succeed, some will be lukewarm, and some will fail.

When you can detach yourself from the results of your experiments, you demonstrate greater resilience, which creates an environment of action. You'll think, "I'll try this. If this does not work, then what is the thing that will work, or where will it lead me?" This exploration leads you to success and achieving your goals on an accelerated timeline, allowing you to blow past your competition.

Another beneficial aspect of leading with a growth mindset is that it reduces the drama around trying new things for yourself and your team. What would you and your team try if they knew there was no penalty for failure? The mental safety that comes from the value of learning is that people are willing to innovate instead of staying in the comfort zone of what is known.

In the journey of entrepreneurship, how you evolve as a person parallels the evolution of your business.

As we've explored, embracing a growth mindset is not just a choice but a necessity in the ever-changing business landscape. Your story, the challenges you've faced, and the transformations you've undergone mirror the metamorphosis of a caterpillar into a butterfly. It's a process that's as inevitable as it is essential.

Your experiences highlight a profound truth: change is constant, but how we respond to it is a choice. By recognizing and shifting from a fixed to a growth mindset, you adapt to change and harness it as a force for growth and innovation. This shift is not a one-off event but an ongoing journey of self-awareness, learning, and adaptation.

Now, it's your turn to reflect and act. Ask yourself: Where do I stand with my mindset? Am I embracing challenges and learning from failures? Am I ready to evolve to meet the demands of my business and personal aspirations?

If you find areas dominated by a fixed mindset, challenge them. Start small, pick one area, and commit to fostering a growth mindset. Remember, it's not about being perfect. It is about progress and persistence.

If you are in a leadership role, think about how you can cultivate this mindset within your team. Encourage innovation, reward effort, and create a safe space for experimentation and learning.

Explore Resilience Through Other Entrepreneur's Stories

Resilience is a key part of being an entrepreneur, and it comes in many forms. By looking at how successful entrepreneurs have stayed resilient, you get real-life examples of how to bounce back and keep pushing forward. Their stories are motivating as they provide practical tips and insights on handling your business's ups and downs.

Simon Cowell: Consider Cowell's journey from school dropout to music industry success, emphasizing his resilience after his first company's failure and his rise to *American Idol* and *X-Factor* fame.

Thomas Edison: Edison's challenges include being deemed unteachable and facing numerous failures, leading to more than 1,000 patents and significant contributions in various fields, showcasing his unwavering commitment to innovation.

J.K. Rowling: Rowling struggled with multiple rejections and personal hardships before achieving monumental success with the Harry Potter series, demonstrating her determination and ability to transform challenges into triumphs.

These stories teach entrepreneurs key resilience lessons: Cowell's tenacity underscores the importance of persistence in career evolution. Edison's story teaches the value of relentless curiosity and learning from failures. Rowling's experience highlights the power of channeling personal struggles into creative success. Emulating these attributes can empower entrepreneurs to transform their challenges into stepping stones for their unique successes.

Their journeys teach us that resilience isn't just about recovering from failures; it's about using these experiences as stepping stones to unparalleled success.

Beyond Business: The Real-World Impact of Resilience

Understanding the tangible benefits of resilience in the business world reveals how this quality transcends beyond personal fortitude, shaping the foundation of entrepreneurial success. Consider these benefits and applications of a resilient attitude:

Improved Decision-Making: Resilience empowers entrepreneurs to view past failures not as setbacks but as invaluable lessons. This mindset fosters a nuanced understanding of risk and decision-making, enabling more strategic and informed choices in future ventures.

Enhanced Crisis Management: A resilient entrepreneur is adept at crisis management. This skill transforms challenges into opportunities, allowing for growth and innovation even in the face of adversity.

Boosted Team Morale: A leader's resilience is infectious. It encourages the entire team with a sense of perseverance and collective strength. This positive culture is crucial in navigating the complexities of team dynamics and maintaining high morale.

Seizing Growth Opportunities: Resilient entrepreneurs are uniquely positioned to capitalize on new opportunities, especially during challenging times. Their adaptability and openness to change enable them to turn potential setbacks into advantageous ventures.

Delving into these real-world impacts of resilience, we see how it benefits individual entrepreneurs and sets the stage for the next phase of our discussion: the enduring journey of resilience in business.

Look Within to See the Benefits of Resilience

Entrepreneurs need to engage in self-reflection to explore the multifaceted benefits of resilience. One effective method is creating a personal timeline of your entrepreneurial journey, marking significant moments of success and failure. Reflect on these pivotal points, focusing on the "bounce-back" moments—how did you feel at the time, and what strategies did you employ to overcome these challenges? Consider what your current self would advise your past self, armed with hindsight and experience. Do not use these moments to give shame, blame, or guilt. Use them to create a better path forward. You did the best you could as you knew it. Now, you know more and can do more.

This exercise isn't just about reminiscing. It is a powerful tool for self-discovery and growth. Acknowledging and learning from these experiences, you can gain valuable insights into your resilience patterns. How did each challenge contribute to your growth? What strengths emerged from these experiences? This analysis will help you recognize and reinforce your resilience strategies, bettering you for future challenges.

By conducting this self-reflection, you fortify your entrepreneurial spirit, turning past experiences into lessons that strengthen your resilience. This self-awareness helps you survive and thrive in the dynamic business world.

Building a Resilient Business Framework

As you work on incorporating resilience into your business framework, consider using defensive and offensive strategies.

Defensive practices protect, preserve, and stabilize your business. Ask questions like: What does your business need to protect the most? As we've outlined, your finances, intellectual property, people, and even one precious resource you may forget to list: *you.* As the business owner, you are an irreplaceable resource in the business until you are out of daily operations and strategic decision-making.

Your health and well-being must be considered to make your company successful. Growth has a habit of being hard on you, leading to burnout. The hustle-and-grind nature of the business also contributes to the problem until there's nothing left and you are ready to throw in the towel.

Putting your life on hold with these two forces at play is exceedingly easy. However, it is self-defeating. You simply can't put your life on hold or allow your business to hold it hostage for the promise of future success. One of the most poignant realizations of the hidden costs of placing my business first in line came during the transition between my first business and Your Biz Rules.

I had volunteered to chaperone a field trip to the zoo with one of the boys. After arriving at the zoo and getting instructions from the teacher, my son, his friend, and I started our exploration. Hanging out behind them, I overheard their conversation.

"Where's your mom?" my son asked.

"She was too busy to come." Sensing his friend's disappointment, my son put his arm around his friend and said, "Yeah, my mom used to be busy, too."

That one comment went straight to my heart. I had no idea my children felt my lack of presence that deeply. I had been too busy for them with the first business. I let the business dominate my every waking moment. The truth I learned from the difference between managing my first business and this one. The one I impart to every business owner with a similar struggle is very simple:

Busyness Does Not Make a Good Business.

There are moments of focus and launch, and then there should be intentional moments of rest and recovery, with things returning to a normal pace in between. Small habits and intentionality make all the difference to a healthy work-life balance.

For instance, let's talk about one of the most stressful things for business owners to do: take a vacation. The stress of getting out the door and the avalanche of responsibilities waiting for you to return. Reentry is enough to undo all the relaxation of a two-week vacation and make you think twice about doing it again. Have you ever wondered if there is another way? We think so.

As a team, Your Biz Rules values vacations for ourselves and for the other people who work in the company. We know that they relieve stress, which brings back a stress-free workspace. With some preparation and a change in expectations, leaving for a vacation can feel good, and returning can be pleasant. It's about setting your intention to make it happen.

The result? More than one of our clients has left their business for a month-long respite this year. In fact, two of our team members are doing the same this year. Would you be able to do the same for yourself? Could you build a culture that supports a month's departure from anyone on the team? What would need to be in place to make it happen?

When we think of defensive practices, it's easy to consider protecting against the negative, but it is equally important to defend the upside.

Conduct honest evaluations of your business vulnerabilities. Is it your team, market, or financial structure? Develop comprehensive plans to mitigate potential obstacles. Build up cash reserves and ensure you have appropriate insurance coverage. Create backup systems and processes that your team can implement. Improve your delegation skills and foster the team's capability of managing operations in your absence. Ensure that your business has continuity by creating a clear outline of who will take over key roles within your business when you are unavailable.

By implementing offensive strategies to build resilience, you do more than protect your business from downturns—you prepare it to seize opportunities and excel, even in uncertain times. Here's how you can adopt these strategies to fortify and expand your enterprise:

Proactively Seek Growth

What if growth and change became the routine? Consider the impact of changing the viewpoint shift. What if you could look beyond your daily operations? Would you invest in new technologies, explore new markets, or develop innovative products? Stay ahead of trends and disruptions, ensuring your business remains relevant and competitive.

Expand Your Network

Strengthen your business by building solid relationships with suppliers, customers, and partners. These connections can provide opportunities and essential support during challenging times. A reliable supplier network, for example, can help maintain your supply chain even when others face disruptions.

Embrace Digital Transformation

Digitize your operations to enhance your business's flexibility. Automate routine tasks, use cloud computing for efficient data management, and expand your e-commerce capabilities. This digital backbone will help your business operate smoothly, regardless of physical limitations.

Develop a Versatile Team

Invest in training your employees to handle multiple roles or work remotely. This flexibility is invaluable in maintaining operations during unexpected disruptions, ensuring your team can adapt and continue delivering without missing a beat.

Secure Financial Flexibility

Arrange for financial safety nets like lines of credit before they're needed. Having these resources ready ensures you can respond swiftly to unexpected situations without financial strain.

Plan for Scalability

Prepare your business to scale up or down efficiently based on market demands. This agility allows you to adjust quickly to opportunities and challenges, maintaining operational efficiency and financial health. We will discuss this more in our closing chapter.

By embracing these offensive strategies, you're doing more than just safeguarding your business. You are setting the stage for dynamic growth and ensuring your business is a resilient, thriving entity ready to capitalize on new opportunities that arise, even in the face of adversity.

Forging Ahead:
Turning Resilience into Sustained Growth and Success

As we wrap up this exploration of resilience, we've equipped you with the tools and insights to survive and thrive amid challenges. From understanding the criticality of a growth mindset to implementing strategies that safeguard and enhance your business's adaptability, you are now prepared to navigate the storms while charting a course toward sustained growth and success.

Let's focus on the next big leap on your entrepreneurial journey. In the upcoming chapter, we begin bridging the gap between resilience and scaling your business effectively—without burnout and while maintaining profitability. Let's set the stage for a future where you scale rich, not just in finances but in fulfillment and freedom.

Chapter 13

LEVEL UP
Scaling Your Business for Maximum Profit

"Scaling doesn't just mean growing bigger.
It means growing better."
—Marc Benioff, CEO of Salesforce

Congratulations! You've laid a strong foundation for your business's growth. Throughout this book, you've learned key concepts laying the groundwork for effectively scaling your business. You've taken the first steps toward sustainable success by focusing on high-impact strategies, refining your leadership skills, and building resilient systems. What if you could harness these lessons to generate more profits effortlessly? It's time to dive into scaling your business.

With the proper foundation in place, scaling becomes significantly easier. Many businesses work tirelessly to prepare: they refine their procedures, expand their teams, and make strategic adjustments to ensure profitability and sustainability. All their diligent efforts culminate in the scaling phase.

Are you ready? Let's examine the various facets of your business and explore the steps to achieve scalable growth.

The Importance of Recognizing Your Business Stage:
Growth vs. Scaling

The challenge lies in knowing whether you're in a growth phase or ready for scalability. Misjudging this crucial distinction can lead to wasted resources, operational inefficiencies, and missed opportunities. That's why it's important to recognize your business stage and choose the right strategy at the right time.

Scaling and growing a business may seem like similar concepts, but they represent different stages and strategies of business development. Think of growth as nurturing a thriving garden while scaling optimizes a high-performing machine.

Growth typically refers to expanding business operations by increasing revenue, adding new customers, or launching new products. It's about building a foundation for expanding the business you've established.

When most entrepreneurs think of scaling, they immediately jump to business growth metrics: more customers, higher revenues, and expanded market share.

Scaling, however, focuses on increasing revenue without substantially increasing costs. It's about optimizing and streamlining operations to handle an influx of customers or projects with minimal additional resources. Plainly stated, scaling is an opportunity to to increase profits easily.

To determine what stage you are in, evaluate your business's current stage and objectives. You're in the growth phase if you're still establishing a customer base or testing new products. However, it's time to scale if you have a solid foundation and want to handle increased demand efficiently.

In Chapter 10, we introduced the theory of the organizational life cycle by describing the development of the business in terms of infancy, teenage, adult, and retirement. With scalability, we are going to take that concept further. Instead of thinking about the cycle as an S, let's think of it as a circle. That circle comprises three phases: growth, scalability, and recovery. Think of these circles as links on a chain, repeating the phases repeatedly. Each link tells a different story. In your first link, your growth phase was longer than the scalability phase, and the recovery phase was even smaller. In the next link, perhaps, the scaling phase was the longest, and in the third link, the recovery phase was the longest. In this way, all phases are important, but perhaps not equal or identical.

We begin to understand the relationship between the three phases is fluid. Setting foundations, growth, and scalability are related to each other. You can't have one without the other. You must go through them in order. Good foundations enable growth. Even with good foundations, growth is inefficient and messy yet necessary for scalability. Scalability is about gaining efficiency and profit. Then what happens after a period of scalability? Maybe you need a phase of rest and recovery to catch your breath and decide what the next level looks like in your vision. You likely need to improve a foundation and then head to another growth phase, followed by the opportunity for scalability.

In this period, with profit plans and good cash-flow-management habits, your periods of scalability should fund your next period of growth. And this is where the magic happens. You accelerate the upward spiral of momentum and goodness, which makes each link of the chain easier to build.

This book has served to bring clarity and understanding to growth, so your journey is one of ease, not struggle. However, it is easy to mistake growth for scaling and vice versa. This can lead to common pitfalls that will slow down your business.

Avoiding Common Pitfalls in Misidentifying Growth and Scaling

Although the terms "growth" and "scaling" are often used synonymously, there is a big difference between the two and the repercussions they have if you get them mixed up.

Inefficient Resource Allocation

If your business focuses on growth when it should be scaling, you may invest heavily in expansion without optimizing operations. This ineffi-cient resource allocation can lead to wasted resources and inefficiencies. For example, imagine a growing restaurant expanding to a second location without streamlining its kitchen processes. The result might be higher costs without a proportional increase in revenue, putting strain on the business.

Operational Overload

On the other hand, if you try to scale before your business is ready, you may overwhelm your existing systems and operations, leading to breakdowns or a decline in service quality. Think of a boutique bakery that suddenly tries to fulfill large wholesale orders without enhancing its production capabilities. It would not surprise me to see delayed orders and customer dissatisfaction damaging the business's reputation.

Stunted Growth

If you focus on scaling prematurely, you might miss crucial growth opportunities, hindering your development. For example, a small software company might focus on automating its sales process before thoroughly understanding its customer base and sales process. This could lead to stagnation, as the company fails to attract new clients or develop new products, missing out on potential growth.

Financial Instability

Mistaking growth for scaling or vice versa can also result in financial instability, as the business might need more revenue or profit to sustain its operations. Imagine a clothing brand that expands its product line without managing production costs, leading to cash flow problems or unsustainable losses. This financial instability can threaten the business's survival.

Misaligned Strategies

Focusing on the wrong phase can result in misaligned strategies that don't align with the business's needs or goals. For instance, a consulting firm might implement advanced scaling strategies like outsourcing before solidifying its core services, leading to inefficiencies or reduced quality. This misalignment can prevent the business from achieving its objectives.

Burnout and Overwhelm

Lastly, focusing on the wrong phase can lead to burnout and overwhelm for both business owners and their teams. Consider a tech startup that pushes for aggressive growth without the necessary systems or support. The result might be stress, burnout, and high turnover, further hindering the business's progress.

The Key Areas of Focus in Moving from Growth to Scaling

As you move from growth to scaling, the key areas of your business—marketing, sales, team, profits, and cash flow—stay the same, but the challenges within each area change significantly. Let's look at each one of these key areas to understand where you are and see if you are ready to scale your business.

Marketing: Reaching and Engaging Customers

Marketing is about attracting and engaging with your customers. You're likely in a growth phase if you struggle to get noticed or differentiate yourself from competitors. You're ready to scale if you're focused on maintaining brand consistency while expanding your reach.

Sales: Converting Leads and Building Relationships

Sales revolve around converting leads and building relationships with customers. You're in a growth phase if you're refining your sales process and struggling with inconsistent conversions. You're ready to scale if you're managing increased demand and focusing on streamlining sales operations.

Team: Building and Managing Your Workforce

Your team is the backbone of your business. If you're building a team that aligns with your vision and fostering a cohesive culture, you're in a growth phase. You're ready to scale if you maintain cohesion while managing a growing team and complex operations.

Operations: Streamlining and Optimizing Processes

Operations, systems, and processes are about creating efficiency and capacity. You're in a growth phase if you're focused on creating predictable delivery and building capacity. If you're handling increased complexity and optimizing efficiency, you're ready to scale.

Profits: Achieving and Maximizing Financial Success

Profits are your business's financial health. You're in a growth phase if you're focused on achieving profitability and managing costs. If you're maximizing profits and increasing efficiency, you're ready to scale.

Cash Flow: Creating and Enhancing Financial Flexibility

Cash flow is the lifeblood of your business. You're in a growth phase if you need to create a predictable cash flow and form a profit plan. If you are ready to optimize cash flow and leverage advanced strategies, you're ready to scale.

Know When it is Time to Move Forward

These key areas form the foundation of your business, and navigating the transition requires a strategic approach. If you need help with issues like inconsistent conversions, growing team complexity, or inefficient cash flow management, you should refine your strategies to ensure sustainable scaling.

However, many entrepreneurs hold themselves back even after identifying these challenges. This hesitation often comes from playing small, from doubts that prevent them from taking bolder actions that could unlock their business's full potential. The tendency to play small is rooted in fears and limiting beliefs that keep entrepreneurs tethered to familiar yet restrictive strategies. Understanding this mindset and how it manifests can reveal why business owners remain stuck in a growth phase instead of embracing the possibilities of scaling.

The Tale of the Flea: A Lesson in Potential

Imagine, if you will, a flea. Not just any flea, but one with the incredible ability to leap distances and heights that, if scaled to human size, would mimic Superman leaping a building in a single bound. This flea represents pure potential, unbound and limitless.

In an intriguing experiment, scientists sought to understand the full extent of this flea's capabilities. They placed it within a glass gallon pickle jar—one with those gold lids that screw on tight. At first, when the flea was introduced to the jar, it performed as expected: it jumped effortlessly out of the jar.

Curious to see what would happen, the scientists placed the flea back inside the jar but twisted the lid on tightly this time. They sat back and observed. The flea, true to its nature, jumped. But this time, it met an unexpected barrier. It struck the lid with a sharp *<ping>*. One could almost hear the echo of its tiny headache. Undeterred, it jumped again, hitting the lid with another *<ping>*.

After a moment to recover, the flea adjusted. It jumped again, slightly lower, just shy of the lid's height. This adjustment, this small act of self-preservation, marked a significant change.

The scientists, now deeply engrossed in their observation, decided to remove the lid and see what would happen. Would the flea remember its full potential? They watched, breath held in suspense.

Yet, the experiment took an unexpected turn. Even with the lid removed, the flea continued to jump just below the previous height of the lid. It never again reached the heights it once effortlessly soared to. The barrier, once physical, had become psychological. Unbeknownst to itself, the flea was now confined to a space below its true potential.

Much like the lessons in this book, the story serves as a metaphor for the invisible lids we often place on ourselves and our businesses. Many entrepreneurs operate under a metaphorical lid, limiting their growth and potential without realizing it.

Our journey together intends to remove these lids, liberate you and your business from the constraints that prevent you from reaching your full potential, and stop playing small when you are built to leap magnificently. Like the flea, you have the inherent capability to reach extraordinary heights. We aim to ensure you remember the lid is gone, encouraging you to leap without bounds and achieve what you truly are capable of.

Understanding the Fear of Playing Small

When business owners hear the word "scaling," they often feel excitement and uncertainty. The promise of exponential growth, increased revenue, and wider impact is enticing, but scaling also means stepping out of the familiar and into the unknown. This step into new territory often reveals the hidden fears that cause many entrepreneurs to play small and hold back.

Some of the most common fears include the uncertainty of taking risks, fear of failure, or concern that scaling too fast could lead to burnout or financial instability. Deep-rooted beliefs can hold us back, stemming from past experiences where bold decisions led to disappointment or from self-doubt whispering that we're not ready or worthy of greater success.

This mindset of playing small can also stem from scaling challenges, like relinquishing control, investing resources, and entering a competitive market. Entrepreneurs who want to maintain high standards and perfectionism often fear delegating tasks to others, thinking only they can get it right.

By holding back, we deny our businesses their full potential and limit our opportunities. We keep our visions in a box, convinced that staying small is safer than risking failure. But the reality is that we have the creativity, skills, and drive to build something extraordinary.

Overcoming This Fear

We've all been there, second-guessing ourselves and underestimating our own potential. Playing small feels safe and comfortable. It shields us from failure, rejection, or scrutiny. But it also traps us in a space where our dreams shrink and our ambitions stagnate.

In doing so, we deny our businesses the opportunity to grow to their fullest potential. We limit our growth and the opportunities for those we serve. We deprive the world of our unique impact, solutions, and vision. The truth is you have the skills, creativity, and drive to build something extraordinary.

So, how do you release your business and yourself from playing small?

1. Acknowledge and Challenge the Fear

Start by recognizing where your limiting beliefs are rooted. Identify the fears holding you back and challenge them. Is your business ready for the next step, but you're afraid of failure? Are you worried about scaling because you feel unqualified or unprepared? Write these fears down, then counter them with facts proving you're capable and ready.

2. Reconnect with Your Vision

Remind yourself of the larger purpose and vision that drove you to start your business. Focus on the positive impact you're here to make, the lives you'll improve, and the change you'll bring. Let this vision guide you forward, even if the path isn't always clear.

3. Surround Yourself with Support

Build a network of mentors, peers, and partners who believe in your potential and offer guidance. Learn from those who've successfully overcome similar challenges, and let their experiences inspire you to think bigger.

4. Take Incremental Risks

Start by making bold, incremental decisions that push your boundaries. Try a new marketing strategy, delegate tasks, or invest in technology. As each small success builds, you'll gain the confidence to embrace larger opportunities.

5. Trust in Your Unique Journey

Remember that every business journey is different. Trust in your path, your timing, and your progress. Focus on continuous improvement and learning rather than measure your growth against others.

Your business has the potential to do amazing things, to transform not just your life but the lives of countless others. Release your fears, embrace your vision, and trust in the value you bring to the world. Step boldly into the possibilities ahead and let your business shine brightly on its unique path to greatness.

Embrace the Possibilities in Your Journey

Pause for a moment. Reflect on how far you've come in your journey. You've faced challenges, navigated obstacles, and kept going even when the path was uncertain. Look at what you've built—an incredible business with the power to change lives, starting with your own.

Remember those bold decisions that paid off, the partnerships that became the bedrock of your success, and the creative ideas that set you apart. These are proof of your vision, your tenacity, and your unyielding spirit. You're shaping a business that can thrive without compromising the life you want to lead.

The dream of scaling is within your reach. You have the determination, experience, and courage to unlock new levels of prosperity and fulfillment. You've laid the groundwork already. With each step forward, you're creating a path that balances ambition with personal joy.

Once you break free from the mindset of playing small, the possibilities of scaling your business await. Imagine a business that works seamlessly, where a well-supported team is empowered to excel, and where you can dedicate time to the relationships and activities that enrich your life. The key is recognizing that growth doesn't have to come at the cost of personal fulfillment.

Embrace the idea that scaling your business is possible and fully within reach. You have the experience, determination, and courage to unlock new levels of prosperity while creating a legacy. Let go of past limiting beliefs and embrace the possibilities with confidence and vision.

Picture the future you're building: A seamless business, a team that supports one another, and a lifestyle that lets you spend quality time with those who matter most. Hold that vision close.

So, take a deep breath and embrace this next chapter of your business. You've got what it takes to make this business the powerful force it's destined to be. The possibilities are limitless, and they're waiting for you.

Step into this new horizon and own the life you've been envisioning. Your best days are ahead.

You've reached this pivotal point where the horizon expands, and you stand at the edge of change. You've come so far, overcoming challenges and establishing a business that's more than resilient—it's poised for growth. With every strategy and system you've honed, you're ready to take the next step: scaling your success.

The journey you've taken through this book laid a strong foundation, helping you build resilience, hone your leadership, and prioritize impactful strategies.

Now, you're primed to embrace the possibilities that *Scaling Rich*™ offers.

IF YOU LIKED THIS BOOK...

In our next book, *Scaling Rich™: Creating Predictable Profits to Grow Your Business without Burnout,* we share how to scale your business efficiently and profitably while upholding your core values. *Scaling Rich* is crafted to resonate with every entrepreneur. It details Alex's journey as he scales his business without compromising what's important to him.

Imagine running a business where everything operates smoothly, your team is thriving, and every decision enhances the company along with your most valued relationships and experiences. In *Scaling Rich,* you'll learn to pinpoint the perfect moment to shift from growth to scaling, maximize your profits, and improve cash flow, stepping up as a visionary leader who transcends daily tasks.

Scaling Rich introduces a fresh perspective on growth beyond boosting revenue or market share. It's about creating a business that succeeds financially and enriches your personal life, offering a sustainable alternative to the relentless hustle culture. It aligns your business ambitions with your personal values and life goals.

You'll uncover advanced strategies to enhance your operational efficiency and profitability, apply savvy financial tactics to fund your growth, and intelligently invest in ways that further your company's goals. These strategies lay the groundwork for a business that serves your ambitions and supports the life you love.

Get ready to transform your business and personal life approach with *Scaling Rich.* This book provides a comprehensive blueprint for achieving prosperity and enriching the relationships and experiences that mean the most to you.

WHEN YOU ARE READY,
WE ARE HERE TO HELP YOU.

219

Ready to get started? If you want to learn more about how we can help you scale your business profitably and successfully, contact us at **https://yourbizrules.com/chat**. We will walk you through each of the foundations of business and fast-track you toward success. We're here to help you achieve your business goals and create a life you love.

INDEX

ABOUT THE AUTHOR

Leslie Hassler is a dynamic author, speaker, business strategist, and founder of Your Biz Rules. Leslie empowers entrepreneurs to cultivate strategies that lead to sustainable growth and increased profitability while avoiding burnout.

With a proven track record in business, finance, mindset, marketing, and entrepreneurship, Leslie's holistic approach has helped businesses across all industries overcome challenges and thrive in a balanced manner. Many business owners who are experts in their field come to Leslie and Your Biz Rules after some measure of success to understand how to run a business that meets their business and their life goals.

Leslie shares her expertise in her books *First This, Then That* and *Scaling Rich*. She has been recognized on stages across the United States, including prestigious events such as the National Association of Women Business Owners and the Women's Business Enterprise National Council. Her insights have also been featured in notable publications like Entrepreneur.com.

Leslie is a mother of two, avid traveler, Past President of NAWBO DFW, and alumni of the Goldman Sachs 10K Small Business program. Leslie is WBENC, HUB, and AI Mastery Certified.

www.ingramcontent.com/pod-product-compliance
Lightning Source LLC
Chambersburg PA
CBHW051515150726
47997CB00001B/259